CHOCOLATE

SO CHIC !

40 chocolate emotions
compiled by
Corinne Decottignies
and illustrated by
Serge Bloch

Corinne Decottignies

Serge Bloch

LA MAISON DU CHOCOLAT
PARIS

CHOCOLATE,
SO CHIC !

ABRAMS | NEW YORK

I come to La Maison du Chocolat
three times a week
to buy a beautiful and glossy rocher,
and I ask them to cut it in half.

I put one half in my mouth,
let it rest on my tongue,
and then let myself
be overwhelmed with ecstasy!

The sweetness of the chocolate,
the freshness of the praline,
and the little almond bits
all melt and blend together in my mouth.
I never chew. I let it all take
its time to inundate my mouth,
and then life is good!

I feel seventy years younger,
I take off, I'm levitating,
gliding, dreaming,
I'm somewhere else,
I'm lost for words...
This is chocolate nirvana
and my taste buds have reached
the promised land.

Enjoying these two ten-minute
pieces of heaven are a sacred act
to match a three-star
fine dining experience
or an embrace with a loved one.
It's love, pure and simple!

I've been buying these sublime
rochers every week for ten years.
I have been unwavering in my loyalty
to this ritual, unable to resist the hold
these enchanting chocolates
have over me. After all,
once you've found paradise,
why would you ever want to leave?

Franck L., chocolate fan, addict, connoisseur and aficionado

40 CHOCOLATE EMOTIONS

They all go loco for cocoa,
gaga for ganache, or even admit
they are completely addicted.
Meet 40 chocoholics who
recount with relish their passion
for the bars they hide in closets,
the energy boosters,
the cocoa antidepressants,
or the indulgence that inspires
their art. Addicts, fans,
connoisseurs, aficionados…
it's completely normal to be
utterly crazy about chocolate!

Fans

Emotion N.1
Mathilde Favier

Emotion N.2
Lindsey Tramuta

Emotion N.3
Lorenz Bäumer

Emotion N.4
Nicolas Cloiseau

Emotion N.5
Irène Cohen

Emotion N.6
**Jérôme
Faillant-Dumas**

Emotion N.7
Léonore Baulac

Emotion N.8
Isabelle Nanty

Emotion N.9
**Danielle
Cillien-Sabatier**

Addicts

Connoisseurs

Aficionados

Emotion N.10
Astier Nicolas

Emotion N.11
Mélanie Laurent

Emotion N.12
Pierre Hermé

Emotion N.13
Ines de la Fressange

Emotion N.14
Audrey Pulvar

Emotion N.15
François du Chastel

Emotion N.16
Nasty

Emotion N.17
Bérangère Loiseau

Emotion N.18
Philippe Labro

Emotion N.19
Sylvia Toledano

Emotion N.20
James Huth

Emotion N.21
Tonino Benacquista

Emotion N.22
Laure Hériard-Dubreuil

Emotion N.23
Jacques Pessis

Emotion N.24
Florence Cathiard

Emotion N.25
Maxime Hoerth

Emotion N.26
Alice et Jérôme Tourbier

Emotion N.27
Hana Lê Van

Emotion N.28
Alain Passard

Emotion N.29
Gilles Descôtes

Emotion N.30
Armen Petrossian

Emotion N.31
Sarah Lavoine

Emotion N.32
Olivier Cresp

Emotion N.33
Kéthévane Davrichewy

Emotion N.34
Carrie Solomon

Emotion N.35
Ramesh Nair

Emotion N.36
Sonia

Emotion N.37
Apollonia Poilâne

Emotion N.38
Dorothée Meilichzon

Emotion N.39
François Nars

Emotion N.40
Catherine, Sylvie, Laurent, Ludovic...

Emotion N.1

MATHILDE FAVIER

Public Relations Manager,
in charge of celebrities worldwide at Christian Dior

Charmingly crAzY cR about ZY CHOCOLATE

When such a slim woman confesses
      her love of chocolate,
            everything we've been led to believe
           goes out the window!

      Mathilde Favier devours chocolate
         in every way.
     With her beautiful wide smile,
        twinkling eyes,

    delicate fingers,
refreshing unpretentiousness,
and a certain self-satisfaction

         given her amazing figure,
             she declares:
      "I eat chocolate
    several times a day."

      But where does she put it all?

        It's very simple:
             everywhere!

Many don't like TO ADMIT IT, *but I like* the **FATTINESS** OF CHOCOLATE

"I can't just say I like chocolate: I'm crazy about chocolate bars, I'm a real chocoholic! I love its sweetness, its creamy fattiness, its density, the way it melts in the mouth, spreads out, and makes you feel almost in-stantly satiated. My day has always started with a 75% pure Ghana chocolate since I was very young. I eat chocolate in all its forms and from all countries: Ecuador, Indonesia, Africa... and at a frequency of one or two squares every couple of hours: it's like happiness medication!"

I love
the sound of
a bar crunching
when I bite!

IT'S PURE ECSTASY WHEN I THINK ABOUT...

A CUP OF HOT CHOCOLATE at ANGELINA's

A YULE LOG at FOUQUET's

CHOCOLATES FROM AU CHAT BLEU in FOUQUET

A WOODEN SPOON CAKED IN CHOCOLATE in my kitchen

A RAGUSA BAR THAT MELTS ON YOUR FINGERS

DARK CHOCOLATE ROCHERS from LA MAISON DU CHOCOLAT

LE BAULOIS CHOCOLATE CAKE I found at the MARKET DE L'ANNONCIATION IN PARIS

My specialty: CHURROS DIPPED IN MELTED CHOCOLATE!

That melting sensation melts the heart!

MY MOTHER's BIRTHDAY CAKE

"I still salivate when I think of the birthday cake mom gave me when I was little girl. It's a simple recipe. Imagine incredibly chocolatey chocolate covered in bright white icing sugar. The contrast, the surprise: sheer pleasure! And it's even better when you know your mother put her heart and soul into it. Nothing beats homemade chocolate cake. Strangely enough, I feel like everyone has her recipe but she's the only one able to make it. This is the one I had on my birthdays:

Melt 9 ounces (250 grams) of bittersweet chocolate with a little water. Emulsify until it's like a thick mayonnaise.

Add 7 ounces (200 grams) of sugar, then 7 ounces (200 grams) of butter which will gently melt in.

Then add 5 egg yolks and 2 level tablespoons of white flour. Fold in very stiff beaten egg whites.

Pour this mixture into a buttered cake tin lined with parchment paper.

FOR THE WHITE FROSTING:

Bake in a preheated 350 °F oven for 20 minutes.

Vigorously mix one egg white and 7 ounces (200 grams) of confectioner's sugar with a spatula. Add the lemon juice and continue beating quickly for 10 seconds.

Once the cake has baked, spread the cake with the frosting."

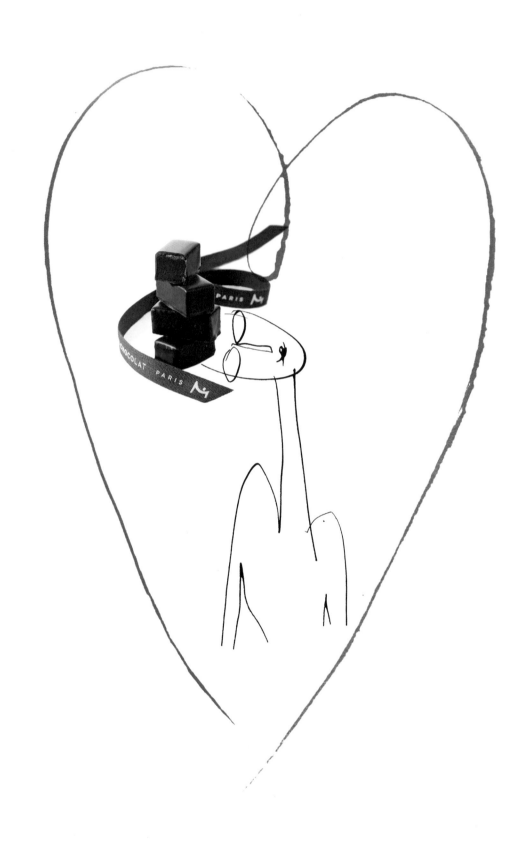

LINDSEY TRAMUTA

Author of *The New Paris*
and @lostncheeseland Instagrammer

PARIS?
LOVE & CHOCOLATE!

Sometimes everything can sound so much
more delicious when described by a foreign foodie.
Lindsey Tramuta is a young American woman
and a talented food writer. She grew up in a country
known for its fast food and thinking the ultimate chocolate
was depicted in *Charlie and the Chocolate Factory*.
But ten years ago she realized that discovering
gastronomy was a very Parisian way of connecting
with the city, and hunting down chocolate
was a great excuse to explore the city!

We are not born *food lovers,* WE BECOME *food lovers*

" I came to Paris for the first time when I was twenty. I realized that if I wanted to truly understand the city, I needed to have expert knowledge of both the language and the food. You can't imagine how intimidating French excellence is when you come from abroad.

I felt like I had to relearn everything from scratch. I walked the streets of Paris and my FIRST SHOCK was all the colors, the creativity, the structures. I went into stores, tasted different foods and then I had my SECOND SHOCK. In fact, it was a revelation:

WHAT I HAD BEEN CALLING CHOCOLATE *before this moment* was not chocolate AT ALL! "

"What was this subtle complexity in the choice of ingredients.

Please explain

Where does the perfect balance come from, the incredible sensations overwhelming the taste buds?"

So how are **FRENCH CHOCOLATES** different?

"French chocolates are simple, refined, and explode in the mouth into complex and intense flavors. I discover new sensations in each chocolate store I walk into."

DIVINE
REVELATIONS

"There are moments of pure ecstasy with chocolate. The Envol collection by Nicolas Cloiseau is like a fresh breath, an untrodden path that leads me to places I would never find by myself, through groves of heady fruit fragrances carried on a gentle breeze. The 'beaux ténébreux' chocolates by Jacques Génin, who tirelessly seeks to generate emotions, give me tingles when I feel their elegance and strength. The singular Patrick Roger, who works chocolate like a raw material, whisks me away to Marie-Galante in the Caribbean before tempt-ing me with the universal allure of a chocolate named Désir. Maybe these artists are the new explorers? You just need to try one of their chocolates to see for yourself."

Paris is chocolate!

—

Paris is good enough to eat. It is lived, eaten, and ingested in every sense. And its story is told through the delicious food it offers. *The New Paris* is Lindsey's new book in which she shares unique insights into the city through the eyes of an American living in Paris.

LORENZ BÄUMER

Jeweler

P R E C I O U S

SOME PEOPLE
HAVE THE
NOBLE PROFESSION
OF CREATING
BEAUTIFUL THINGS
FOR OTHERS.

Lorentz Bäumer is one
such man.
His renowned Paris jewelry store
sits on one of the most
famous squares
of the capital.
This creator of dreams
and wizard with stones
is passionate about
many things:
he loves artists and dreams
that become reality,
sandy beaches
with ephemeral crashing waves,

and, of course,
divine chocolate.
It's only fitting
that for those
that come to see his work
in the privacy of
his home in Place
Vendôme, he offers
a selection of chocolates,
chosen with
as much care
as his precious stones.

66 Chocolate gives access
to pure luxury.
Whenever you taste the
creations of Nicolas Cloiseau
or Alain Ducasse,
you are given irrefutable
proof that luxury
is not all about money. 99

"I like to eat chocolate as I'm walking down the street, looking at the Paris sky with its scattered clouds. Fine chocolates, chocolate tarts... All chocolate opens →

A VIP

"I had the immense privilege of having met Robert Linxe in his first La Maison du Chocolat boutique on rue Faubourg Saint-Honoré. Because I'm a huge fan of chocolate, he invited me on a private tour of his kitchen where we were able to discuss the various virtues of milk chocolate and dark chocolate. It was a passionate debate by two passionate people, during which we mainly talked about emotions. Because that's what it's all about really: the emotion one feels when enjoying a chocolate. A memory of youth, a surprising discovery, an unexpected revelation. As strange as it may seem, I was comparing this experience to when a woman opens a box and sees the jewel inside. It is the emotion felt that is so exhilarating. This is what a jeweler looks for and also what a chocolatier hopes will happen when someone tastes their chocolates. They try to read it in your eyes, they wait for the first word that you use to describe this ineffable pleasure."

visit

Rings by Lorenz Bäumer

" There is a beautiful diamond known as the 'Chocolate'

THE CHOCOLATE DIAMOND

diamond because its color is reminiscent of chocolate. I have created a few pieces of jewelry with this exceptional colored stone.

my mind to creative possibilities.
It allows me to disconnect and to look for images elsewhere, in another world that's delicious, delicate and gourmet all at the same time."

WHEN CHOCOLATE BECOMES VALUABLE, IT'S EVEN HARDER TO RESIST! "

Welcome to the land OF LUXURY

"Because I'm a complete addict and member of the Club des Croqueurs de Chocolat, I serve chocolates to customers and friends in my store on small hand-painted plates from a custom-made dessert table.

It's my way of taking them on a sensual and emotional journey, a journey for those passionate about luxury. Chocolate, like jewelry, is best enjoyed with company."

Emotion N. 4

NICOLAS CLOISEAU

Master Chef of La Maison du Chocolat
Best Craftsman Chocolatier of France

DON'T TELL MY MOTHER I'M AN ARTIST,

SHE THINKS I'M A MOF* AT LA MAISON DU CHOCOLAT!

* Meilleur Ouvrier de France or "Best Craftsman of France"

Is that a blue, white,
and red collar I see?
Proof if ever it were
needed that we're looking at a big shot!
    And not just any old VIP
        because his job
        is to bring joy   to millions: *(who eats more than 13 lb. of chocolate per month!)*

            he is Master Chef
        of La Maison du Chocolat.

    After earning his stripes
    in Lannion in Brittany,
            he sealed his reputation under
            the watchful eye of the illustrious
            Robert Linxe.
                Nicolas Cloiseau's
                incredible
            and visionary
                    creations
                have amazed and surprised
                    in equal measure
                    ever since.

THIS IS WHERE WE LIFT THE LID AND FIND OUT EVERYTHING THERE IS TO KNOW (OR ALMOST) ABOUT THE HEAD CHOCOLATIER CHEF OF LA MAISON DU CHOCOLAT. FROM OUR QUESTIONS AND HIS ANSWERS, WE FIND THAT BEHIND THE CONCENTRATION AND DISCIPLINE, THERE IS A GREAT FONDNESS AND LOVE OF NATURE AND FOR THE SIMPLE THINGS IN LIFE.

NI CO

QUESTIONS

WHAT DO PEOPLE NOT KNOW ABOUT YOU?

I am often surprised that people who come to work at La Maison du Chocolat don't come to the creative workshop to see what goes on there and how one of our creations is made. My work partner, Alexis, tells me that I intimidate them and can seem cold. It's true, sometimes I'm quite guarded and I main-tain this image. So, let's say it once and for all: the chef won't bite, come in!

WHERE WILL YOU BE IN 20 YEARS?

Maybe I'll be a grandfather, or a pro-spective retiree, ready to hand over to my successor. I hope I have the chance to appoint him or her so that La Maison du Chocolat is still faithful to its style, just as Robert Linxe appointed me head of the decoration workshop. It's always strange to think of your future self. I probably won't have any hair left and I'll probably have a few extra pounds with all the chocolate I'll have eaten over the last sixty years!

IF YOU HADN'T BECOME HEAD CHEF OF LA MAISON DU CHOCOLAT, IN WHAT FIELD WOULD YOU HAVE WORKED?

I would have done high-end jewelry. There are so many similarities: the ma-terials, the assembling, the deco-rat-ing of the final piece, the fun, the small molds for melting metals, the luxury, and the absolute need for perfection!

WHO IS YOUR FAVORITE HISTORICAL FIGURE?

Louis XIV. Not for his military or politi-cal actions, but for the boost he gave to all forms of art and culture. True, he spent vast sums of money, but he certainly helped many artists, authors, playwrights, sculptors, and even gar-deners to emerge! He made many mis-takes, but we can partially forgive him. He allowed so many talents to express themselves.

1

LAS

CLOISEAU

WHAT CHOCOLATE HAVE YOU HAD TO GIVE UP TRYING TO INCLUDE IN YOUR COLLECTIONS?

I haven't yet found the right balance to introduce seaweed ganache. I hope one day to be successful with it, but for now we haven't found the right kind of seaweed that meets our criteria.

WHICH IS YOUR FAVORITE CHOCOLATE AT LA MAISON DU CHOCOLAT?

The Quito: a perfectly balanced plain ganache which I never tire of. I also love the Noir du cassis with fruity Burgundy blackcurrant pulp and floral notes. And as for infused chocolates, I have a soft spot for the Zagora with fresh mint leaves.

WHAT DO YOU ALWAYS TAKE WITH YOU ON VACATION?

Chocolate! I bet you weren't expecting that answer!

WHAT IS YOUR BIGGEST FAULT?

I'm never satisfied! So it's hard to be truly delighted. But when I make a compliment, you know you've done well.

AND WHAT'S YOUR BEST QUALITY?

I'm very attentive, very open. You can really count on me to listen, respond, and pay attention to the suggestions of those around me.

WHAT DO YOU LIKE TO INDULGE IN?

Chocolate, in the evening!

WHICH FAMOUS PERSONALITY WOULD YOU LIKE TO BE?

Leonardo da Vinci, the most complete genius of them all: painter, draftsman, botanist, engineer, architect, and much more. I would like the satisfaction of being someone who could explore all their talents and dream.

CHEF'S TIPS

While relentlessly blazing a trail to explore as yet undiscovered regions of the chocolate world, he always finds bold and relevant ways to offer his customers new experiences with this magical food.

Here, Nicolas Cloiseau offers us some little tips to help us turn our family "recipes" into family "secrets."

Chocolate *is* A DOMINANT FLAVOR

"Go easy on the sugar! When making a chocolate cake, use sugar sparingly because it needs to bring out the chocolate and not mask it. If you use too much sugar, the cake will lack flavor. Remember: with sugar, enough is enough!"

Whip *into* SHAPE

"Do you want your chocolate mousse to be lighter but hold its shape better? Here's a little trick that works every time: add whipped cream to your egg whites."

REAL *hot* CHOCOLATE

"A proper hot chocolate is creamy, thick but not too thick, and tastes like chocolate instead of just looking like chocolate. That's what we all want, but often don't find. My secret: use chocolate couverture instead of cocoa powder and simmer over a very low heat. Be patient and you will be rewarded with a creamy, velvety hot chocolate."

Baking chocolate IS NOT ALWAYS THE BEST CHOCOLATE *for baking*

"Baking chocolate has a lower proportion of cocoa butter so it is less fluid and takes more effort to work. Choose couverture chocolate instead. You can find it easily and it's much easier to work with."

Mix *and* MATCH

"We bake and make pastries to please others (and ourselves of course!). The goal is to hear the 'mmmm' sounds and smacking lips that betray pure pleasure. The way to get this reaction is simple: combine several sensations in the same dessert and create surprise by playing with soft, flowing, crunchy, melting, and crispy textures. Then let the magic happen!"

IRÈNE COHEN

Founder of the children's brand and concept store Bonton

Is an Easter Egg Laid by a Chocolate chicken?

Easter is the quintessential
gourmet festival and the one
where, after the egg hunt,

we are allowed to go straight
to dessert before the main
course. The idea of starting
with dessert is something
to celebrate in itself!

HAPPY —
HOLIDAYS

"Toys, soft colors, a magical fantasy world, and all the things we dreamed we could have as a child. This is the universe of Bonton, an escape into a unique world that stimulates the desire to organize family celebrations, make snacks for children, to decorate, drape, and dress up with fun fabrics from all four corners of the world. And when it comes to chocolate, it's this family atmosphere and these celebrations that always spring to mind: little chicks from Maison Chaudun, memories of past Easters —

A FEAST
for
the eyes

"It's fascinating watching kids on an egg hunt: wide eyes searching all around, little legs running everywhere. I kept it up until I was fifteen years old.

My childhood friend Caroline and I, baskets in hand, would always join in the family egg hunt. When our baskets were full of eggs and chocolate, our eyes would already

Boxes, choice, colors, wonderfully creative shapes and decorations: this is what chocolate is all about. Easter chocolate is also about

A GIFT THAT KEEPS ON GIVING

when all the cousins and friends got together for the unforgettable Easter egg hunt. Chocolate-egg-shaped memories!"

surprises, especially that moment when we finally break open the egg to see what's inside. It's like a Russian doll, chocolate inside chocolate, a gift within a gift. And the pretty boxes they all come in have almost become collectibles these days.

have gorged
    themselves,
        but our stomachs
    still had to wait
        for that signal from
        our parents giving
us the go ahead
to devour our loot."

JÉRÔME FAILLANT-DUMAS

Creative Director
and Founder of Love and Love Éditions

A LESSON

IN ⎯⎯⎯⎯⎯⎯

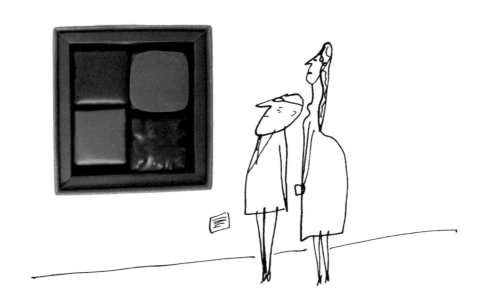

(GOOD) TASTE

IF

perfectionism is one of the fundamental values of luxury, Jérôme Faillant-Dumas is certainly one of its ardent defenders. Nothing slips by his amazing appreciation for perfection and beauty. Along with other creative projects, he designs both contemporary and timeless creations that combine clean lines and simple forms with strong colors. Where does chocolate fit into this? Very few treat chocolate with as much respect as Jérôme Faillant-Dumas. For him, good chocolate perfectly illustrates the perfectionism of major French luxury brands.

THE MEANING *of* chocolate

"Every
chocolate
provides
access
to a very
personal
imagination,

"For me, the emotion I feel with great
chocolate comes from the realization that
a small chocolate bonbon can suddenly
embody a chocolatier, it becomes like a mini-
muse, a symbol in and of itself. Within this
tenth of an ounce, we find all the passion
of a great chocolate house, all its expertise,
its standards, its perfectionism, its creativity...

and I feel
that

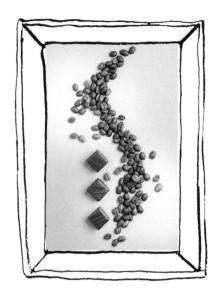

if beauty can
teach us something,
so can
deliciousness."

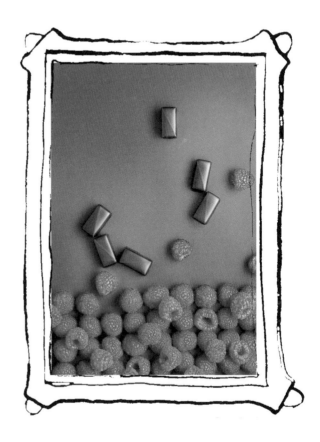

→ And that's what fascinates me: this rigorous pursuit of perfection put into what amounts to a fleeting moment of tasting pleasure."

I LOVE *the* ETIQUETTE *of* CHOCOLATE MAKERS

"The perfect chocolate displays perfect balance, a stylish ribbon, a refined and neat box, embossed paper, a custom-fit bag. Everything gives off an impression of luxury in a kind of timeless osmosis. When we buy something bearing the luxury standards of a major brand, we gain access to their etiquette, their exclusivity. Before tasting, we are already introduced to the sophistication: they serve you with small cotton gloves, and each person in the chocolate shop knows the best vintages as intimately as you know the best work of a great designer or your family secrets. For just a few dollars, you have the privilege of entering into this unique and sensual world. And then you enjoy something exceptional yet so ephemeral. That's the paradox and the beauty of it all. Behind each creation, each chocolate collection, there is a story to uncover and explore."

mayukkuma88

#chicchoc

#chocnflowers 😍

 **jotpot19**
New York, New York

angweddingsny
Central Park Zoo

#instachicetgourmand 🍫🖤

 pandakitchen

Emotion N.7

LÉONORE BAULAC

Prima Ballerina
at the Paris Opera Ballet

CHOCOLATE?
IS ONE
OF MY
WORK
TOOLS!

Great news for those
with a soft spot for chocolate:
you can still be in great shape if you eat
half a chocolate bar (or more!) every day.
So what's the secret?
You have
to dance for nine hours every day!
Yes, unfortunately there's no such
thing as a free lunch. Léonore Baulac,
Prima Ballerina at the
Paris Opera Ballet,
is living proof that we can give in
to temptation while being rigorously
disciplined.
While dance is the focus of her
life, chocolate is a constant partner she can't
say no to and with whom
she practices every day.

BACKSTAGE
↓
BAR

CHOCOLATE
Ritual

"For me, chocolate always brings back memories of when I first arrived at the Paris Conservatoire. I was thirteen and I spent my days between dance and college, with my friend Colombe. We had a ritual: every day we would share a seven-ounce bar of dark chocolate. We would open up the bar during the few breaks in the day we had, unwrap the silver foil and bite into the dark chocolate. We did this for years, until we discovered that there was better chocolate out there: chocolates from fine chocolate makers, chocolates with special flavors... This was the start of my passion for fleur de sel chocolate.

CHOCOLATE IS ONE OF MY WORK TOOLS!"

"I always have chocolate in my dressing room at the opera house. I have dark chocolate, chocolate with almonds, or chocolate with fleur de sel. Chocolate is a great pick-me-up for bouts of exhaustion. ⟶

THE BREAKFAST OF CHAMPIONS

"Every morning I eat chocolate: a bar of dark chocolate dipped into my tea, which then melts in the mouth. I then have another bar, which I break into small pieces and add to my cereal and soy yogurt. It's the best way to start the day and provides the right balance of nutrients I need for work."

My work days are very intense:
I have dance lessons from
eleven in the morning until
noon, then rehearsals directly
after until four in the afternoon,
which means I don't have
a lunch break. So you have
to find ways to fight off fatigue
and keep going until the end.
Chocolate is great for that,
especially with a handful
of almonds. If there's a
performance in the evening,
I have rehearsals again from half
past four until seven o'clock.
If there is a performance, I start
preparing for it straight after
my chocolate/snack break.
There's no time for meals.
To keep up this rhythm,
I need energy and chocolate
provides me with that."

Travel essentials
"Just as I always have chocolate
in my dressing room, I always take
my chocolate bars with me when
I go on tour. I need to have
my supplies with me, it's reassuring.
Then I don't need to try and find
them wherever I am!"

Because of her Norwegian roots, Isabelle Nanty may spontaneously start talking about the unpronounceable yet delicious Kvikk Lunsj bars she remembers from her childhood, but she will happily talk for hours about any chocolate. Hot, cold, crispy, and creamy, chocolate reminds her of a family life where celebrations seemed to revolve around good food. It seems Norway is crazy about chocolate too!

CHOCOLATE-

As a teenager,
I loved praline rochers.
I also loved the chocolates with
'Won' or 'Lost'
under the wrappers,
and Daim candy bars.
These chocolate-flavored
memories are still just as vivid
twenty or thirty years later!

Emotion N.8

ISABELLE NANTY

Actress

—COATED

MEMORIES

DIVINE
REVELATIONS

THE FIRST sip OF CHOCOLATE

Hot chocolate at Christmas! It's such a distinctive flavor AND MEMORIES OF CHILDHOOD COME FLOODING BACK AS SOON AS I TAKE MY FIRST SIP. My father worked for a company that organized A CHRISTMAS PARTY FOR CHILDREN every year. We all gathered in a canteen, which served as a party hall, and we were all given amazing hot chocolate. It was a really chocolatey, thick and creamy hot chocolate. AND WHEN YOU HAD FINISHED THE LAST SIP, THERE WAS ALWAYS A LITTLE MOUND OF CHOCOLATE IN THE BOTTOM OF THE CUP WHICH YOU COULD SCOOP OUT WITH A SPOON. My Norwegian family Christmases also involved a massive box of chocolates brought by my aunt. We would all fight over the same chocolate, and there was only one of them: a small chocolate liqueur cup, wrapped in bright red paper. You always love bright and shiny things when you're young. THAT'S CHOCOLATE FOR ME: LIQUID, SOLID, AND BRIMMING WITH EMOTIONS AND MEMORIES.

While some may remember being raised on Gerber instant cereal, many Norwegians are treated to home-made versions! When I think of my childhood, I remember gluttonous moments with my grandmother's chocolate porridge, which we call Sjokoladegrot - oppskrift. I remember the ingredients because I have often tried to make my own version, without much success (usually too lumpy!). Anyway, it's cocoa powder, whole milk, potato starch, and that's it! Throw all that in a saucepan and heat. My grandmother would heat this

Did I hear you say

SJOKOLADEGRØT - OPPSKRIFT?

mixture up until it became thick and dark. A skin forms on the surface, then you sprinkle brown sugar on top of it and it eventually cracks. The sugar brings out the dark chocolate, which fills the whole house with a delicious aroma. I would smell this sweet chocolate smell and stand in the front of the saucepan, waiting for that moment when I could plunge my spoon into the yummy thick porridge!

#ladouceursucree

#chocolatshowgourmand

alaina_ny

#chocolatchaud

#aboireetacroquer

DANIELLE CILLIEN-SABATIER

Manager of Librairie Galignani, Paris

Book lovers
need only hunt down
one place in Paris:
Librairie Galignani.
If you love
the smell of paper
and wax in a large
oak library,
then this bookstore
has it all.
One cannot
help respecting
and admiring
this historical
monument
to culture and
the written word.

C
HO CO
LATE
is
MY (only)
DRUG

In a quiet office
full of tempting
tomes, we sit
down with Danielle
Cillien-Sabatier
to talk about
chocolate.
Another passion
of hers among all that
this world has to offer,
which inspires particularly
delicious memories...

Gluttony

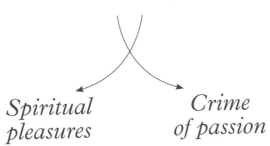

Spiritual pleasures

Crime of passion

"I love the beauty of chocolate: the fabulous packages from Chapon (and their absolutely divine mousse!), the simple yet stylish boxes from La Maison du Chocolat that you never want to throw away, or those from Ducasse (where everything is beautiful!). When I was younger and in preparatory class, I was at boarding school and every week I used to receive a package from my grandmother in Luxembourg. It contained a box of chocolates. It would always give me comfort and pleasure. There's something spiritual about enjoying chocolate when you're alone."

"Chocolate is behind one of the biggest punishments of my life. I was six years old, living in Ivory Coast. My parents worked and I was meant to behave myself at home. Of course, children are preprogrammed to rebel. And when you get a chocolate craving, it's a lost cause trying to resist! So, I made the decision to steal some money from my mother's wallet and walk one mile and across many roads to buy some chocolate from the store. Everything went like clockwork. I returned home and was enjoying my chocolates until I heard an angry voice: 'What have you been doing?' And that's when the trouble started.

The neighbor had seen me go and come back, and had asked mother: 'Where did Danielle go? I saw her leave and not come back until two hours later.' →

DANIELLE CILLIEN-SABATIER

For several years I worked at L'Express in Paris, near the Pleyel opera house and right by Robert Linxe's chocolate boutique. There's nothing worse than working right next to a master chocolatier. I used to buy cakes from there and marvel at what perfectly balanced works of art they were. My mouth starts to water just thinking about it today. Biting into a chocolate cake is an incredible sensory experience: all the colors, layers, textures... Just describing chocolate is gluttony in itself. Attempting to interpret it is quite the intellectual exercise: it's often

THE INTENSITY

—— OF

EPHEMERAL JOY

" Along with flowers and books, chocolate is something I like to give to others.

It's an indulgence that elicits pleasure and that special, intense feeling you only experience from something short-lived. **"**

It's irrational to deny yourself

There's nothing worse than a meddling nosy neighbor next door! I had to own up to what I'd done, but, strangely enough, I don't remember being deprived of chocolate."

difficult to find the right words. Chocolate is my only drug and I can't live without it. Besides, to deny yourself chocolate would entail giving up something that provides comfort, happiness, and energy. And that's simply irrational! Chocolate is the food of the gods!

CHOCOLATE'S TRUE COLORS

↓

Brown, but what kind of brown? A good chocolate should be the color of brown mahogany and have a slight sheen. When buying a big piece of chocolate in some chocolateries, the salesperson sometimes uses a polishing brush to give it some extra shine and bring out all its beautiful details.

A GOOD EYE

Do you have white residue on the surface of your chocolates? There are two possible reasons for this: If moisture comes into contact with the chocolate, it can suffer from "sugar bloom" where sugar is brought to the surface from condensation and then crystalizes. The other type is "fat bloom," where temperature fluctuations can destabilize the cocoa butter molecules, which then separate on the surface. Although harmless, neither type is desirable! The flavor isn't affected, but who wants moldy looking chocolate?

↑

LITTLE WHITE LIE

MATTE
OR
GLOSS?
←

Both please. The art of creating a good chocolate is not to make it too dull or too glossy. You want a "satin" finish, a happy medium between the Millennium Star Diamond and sienna.

FOR GOOD
CHOCOLATE

That is the big question. A fine chocolate has a very smooth coating, which should mean it melts rather than crunches.

↑

CRUNCHY
OR
SOFT?

Emotion N.10

ASTIER NICOLAS

Equestrian
two-time medalist at the Rio Olympics

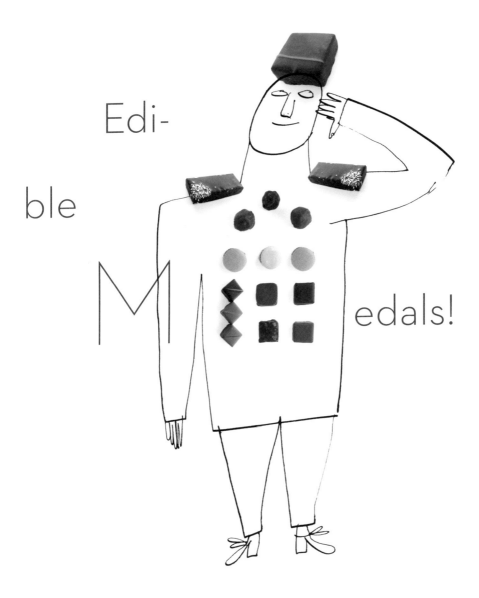

Edi-

ble

M

edals!

Just twenty-seven years old and he already has a trophy haul to rival many riders from around the world. Astier Nicolas became a true riding star in 2016, bringing two medals back from the Rio Olympics: gold in the team eventing and silver in the individual eventing. His passion for winning is obvious to those who meet him, but it turns out he also loves another kind of medal— of the chocolate variety!

CHOC

STOCKS

"My stables were in England for three years so I had to adapt my chocolate habits. The English love rum-filled chocolates and it's very hard to find good plain chocolates. Fortunately, I regularly had to go back to France for competitions so I could stock up on chocolate.

NOW I ALWAYS HAVE SOME ON ME BECAUSE CHOCOLATE IS GREAT FOR ATHLETES. ALL YOU NEED IS A LITTLE BITE TO MELT IN YOUR MOUTH AND YOU'LL NEVER LOSE!"

GOLD
is great,
but
I'll also
settle
FOR CHOCOLATE

"When you're
a rider, you dream
of medals.

When you enter
competitions, you're given
satin rosettes and plaques
bearing the name of the
events you've just won. But
you only win medals at major
sporting events.

So everyone knows
what it means
to win a medal,
even the younger
riders who compete
are at the French
Championships
in Lamotte-Beuvron.

But there are other special
medals, not as prestigious
perhaps, but just
as appealing: chocolate
medals, four inches
in diameter, from Crins
d'Or! All the chocolates
from this chocolatier are
shaped around the theme
of equestrian competition—
it is true chocolate for
champions. I won this
famous chocolate medal
for the first time last year
in a competition.

I thought
winning
a chocolate
medal
was
a bit of
an insult, until
I bit into
it!

Now I always have some on
me because

chocolate is great
for athletes.
All you need
is a little bite to melt
in your mouth
and you'll
never lose!"

theexceptionalwhisky

 krissharv3y
SLS Hotel at Beverly Hills

#urbanchocs 🍫👍🤍💕🍫

MÉLANIE LAURENT

Director and actress

EMOTIONAL RESP o NSES

We subject Mélanie Laurent to a Proust questionnaire to see what some simple questions and answers can reveal about her passion! She takes you on a journey into her childhood memories where chocolate looked like the Queen of Sheba.

YOUR FAVORITE CHOCOLATE? → ←

"Milk chocolate, with a creamy ganache, and what I love most of all: chocolate with marzipan. That's my weakness! It's a heavenly combination, guaranteed to make your mouth water!"

BEST TIME FOR CHOCOLATE? → ←

"As an after-school snack. Even these days it's still the best moment to indulge. The fun of being a kid, that moment we get back home and look what's on the table: nice bread, chocolate, fruit juice... Oddly enough, everyone becomes strangely obedient at times like this when you tell them to sit down at the table for their snack!"

CHOCOLATE BONBONS OR A CHOCOLATE BAR? →

← "Chocolate bonbons for sure! Although both are very different. But chocolates bonbons are defi-nitely my absolute favorite, with all the different types, the surprises, and sometimes disappoint-ments too, especially when you come across one you don't like! Then you're allowed to have anoth-er one so you can end on a good note. Even if the door to pleasure is opened through deception, we all win!"

WHO DO YOU GIVE THEM TO? AND WHEN? →

← "My life is like I'm constantly traveling. I'm very lucky because I've been able to discover some amazing places and all that France has to offer. One of these discoveries is undoubtedly chocolate. It's part of French culture. Everything made from good chocolate is always special. When I travel, I always try to bring back some for all my friends, especially the chocolate macaroons from La Mai-son du Chocolat. These are always something I have to indulge in and introduce people to."

HOT CHOCOLATE OR ICED COFFEE? → ←

"Hot chocolate, very very hot! Because you need to start your mornings with something sweet. And for a snack, to bring back childhood memories and enjoy a moment when it's not naughty to have something sugary."

A FAMILY RECIPE? ⟶ ⟵ "Queen of Sheba cake, no question.
I used to make it with my grandmother when I was a little girl. As a kid,
as soon as we get out a bowl, it's the big league. You feel like you're being
a great pastry chef. You use all your energy to break up the chocolate bar
and mix with the wooden spoon, alt-hough you're actually waiting for the
best bit: when you get to lick the bowl and spoon afterwards!"

SHARE OR SELF-INDULGE? ⟶ ⟵ "Probably both. Although
cooking and food in general are for sharing above all."

" Chocolate:
it has a soft, tender,
and sweet heart,
with lots of
body
and character.
Sounds like
the perfect description
of someone you could
fall in love with! "

Mélanie's *grandmother's* QUEEN of SHEBA Cake

SHOPPING LIST

- 3 eggs
- 4 oz. (125 g) butter
- 4 oz. (125 g) dark chocolate
- 4 oz. (125 g) powdered sugar
- 2 oz. (60 g) almond flour
- 2 tablespoons flour

LET'S GET COOKING!

Combine the butter and chocolate in a bowl. Melt them gently using a water bath. When the mixture turns "liquid," add the powdered sugar and almond flour.

Then add the flour and mix well. Off the heat, mix in three egg yolks, then add the beaten egg whites.

Spoon this mixture out into a buttered cake pan, then bake for 25 minutes at about 300 °F.

Remove from the pan while still warm. Then shout out to everyone:

WHO WANTS CAKE?!!!

Emotion N.12

PIERRE HERMÉ

Pastry chef

THE
SORCERER'S
APPRENTICE

THE GREAT THING ABOUT A GREAT CHEF IS THAT THEY ALWAYS KNOW HOW TO SURPRISE.

Pierre Hermé is no exception to the rule. While he was searching his past for a memory full of chocolate emotions, he realized

" To get the full experience of a trade, you need to be interested in its evolution and in those who contributed to it. "

that there was no chocolate named after the sorcerer of ganache, Robert Linxe, founder of La Maison du Chocolat. So he paired a symbol of the house's past with the house of today by creating his own recipe, one that paid tribute to the man who had been his inspiration since he first became a chef.

THE INCOMPA-RABLE ROBERT LINXE!

"This great man was a source of inspiration for me, and without him, the world of chocolate would never have been what it is today. Robert Linxe was the embodiment of passion for chocolate, and not only dark chocolate. He also loved milk chocolate and defended its greatness as a purist. He also had this incredible ability to create exceptional ganache with very fragile products. There isn't a chocolatier who hasn't been inspired, in one way or another, by his work, his technique, or his exploration of flavors and sensations. All chocolatiers who have experienced his chocolates from La Maison du Chocolat have said at some point: 'How did he do that?' It was high time I paid tribute to him in a sincere and simple way, in his own domain, with the ingredients he loved using to surprise and delight food lovers everywhere.

AND HERE IS MY HUMBLE POSTHUMOUS DEDICATION: THE ROBERT GANACHE! Because chocolate is always an emotion, something to share and pass on."

Translation : Page 191

PIERRE HERMÉ

12 RUE FORTUNY   PARIS 17e

BONBON CHOCOLAT "ROBERT"

12mm — ganache pure origine Belize 64%
2mm
chocolat à l'amarante

enrobage chocolat noir

marquage fourchette carrée + rouge

Ganache Pure origine Belize 64%

650 g de crème
700 g de Couverture chocolat
    pure origine Belize 64%
40 g glucose DE60
115 g de beurre

CHOCOLAT A L'AMARANTE

500 g de couverture chocolat Pure Origine "Belize 64%
80 g de beurre clarifié
55 g d'amarante grillé (160°C → 20 min)

Etaler à 2 mm, laissez prendre/cristalliser puis couler la
ganache par dessus à 12mm
Detailler à 30m x 15mm

12/05/2016

Emotion N.13

INES DE LA FRESSANGE
Fashion designer

THERE'S NO
SUCH THING AS
BAD TASTE
IN
CHOCOLATE

Can you believe it?
Ines de la Fressange, the quintessential Parisian,
is a huge chocolate fan! And as you
would expect from such a unique and
surprising woman, she doesn't like the kind
of chocolate you'd expect! Iconic milk-chocolate
Toblerones, super-sweet chocolate candy bars...
It's even more chic and glamorous when it's completely
unexpected. It's proof that there's no such thing
as bad taste in chocolate.
When she isn't drawing inspiration from chocolate,
she's drawing charming little sketches
that inspire others to be who they want to be.
When French chic is so chocolate...

5 delectable drawings

Translation: Page 191

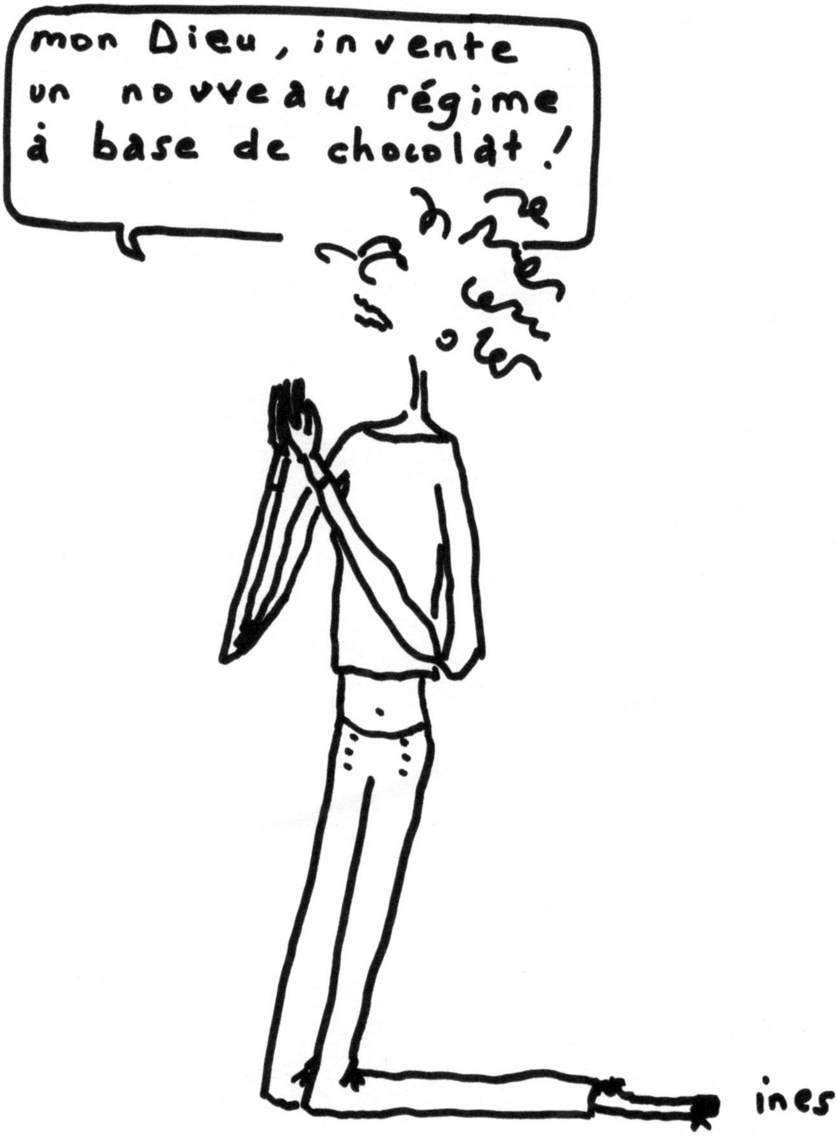
mon Dieu, invente un nouveau régime à base de chocolat !
ines

24 RUE DE GRENELLE
75007 PARIS

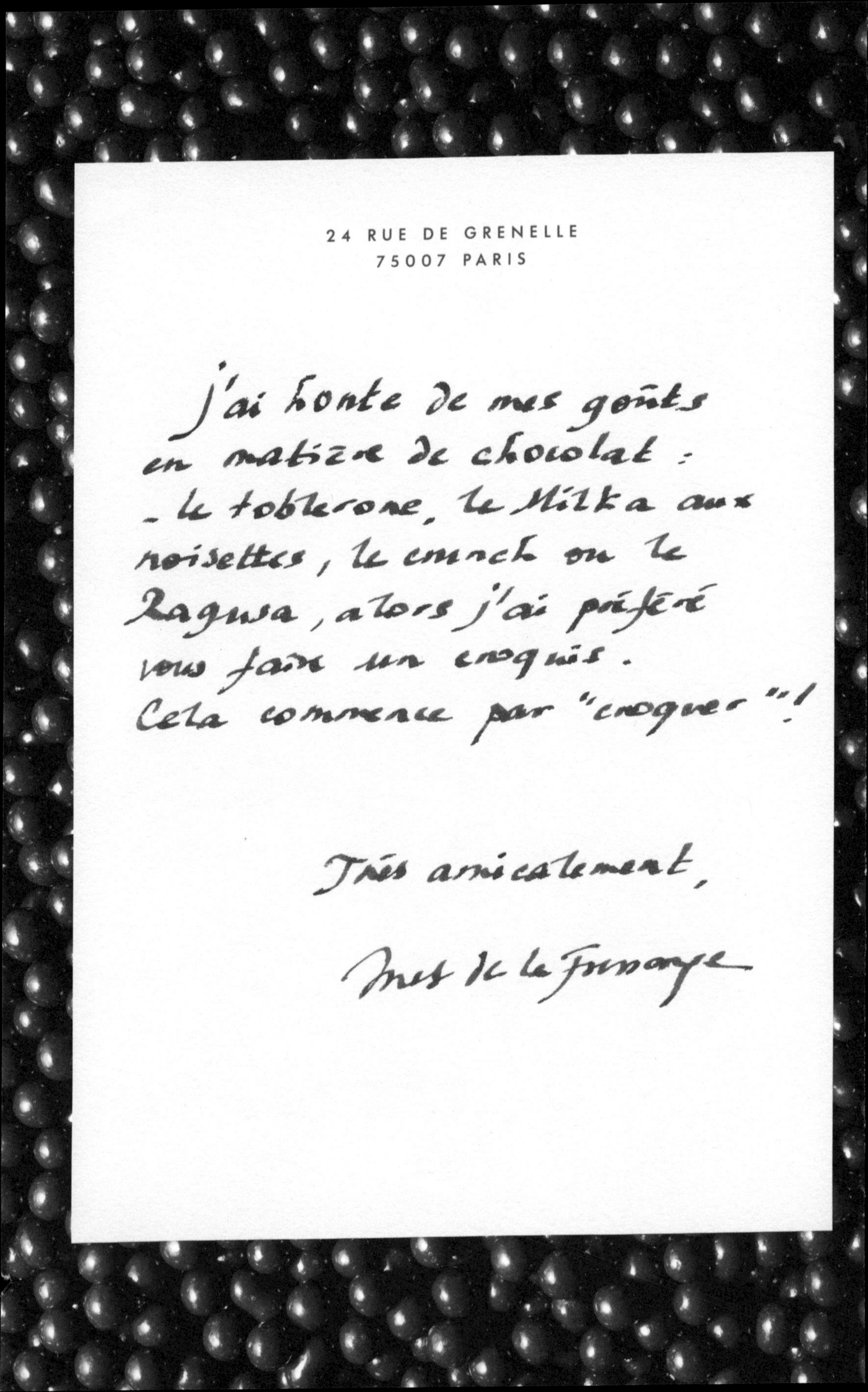

J'ai honte de mes goûts
en matière de chocolat :
– le toblerone, le Milka aux
noisettes, le crunch ou le
Ragusa, alors j'ai préféré
vous faire un croquis.
Cela commence par "croquer" !

Très amicalement,

Inès de la Fressange

Emotion N.14

AUDREY PULVAR

Journalist

PARIS:
The Ultimate
RELIGIEUSE
_AU_ *CHOCOLAT*

For Audrey Pulvar, chocolate is a passion. It brings back memories of childhood and has been the destination of many a food adventure. While she loves it in all its classic forms, she is also a big fan of discovering new chocolate sensations, for chocolate is always an intense experience for Audrey!

Travel broadens the mind

"A fond memory of chocolate? I remember coming to Paris for the first time when I was seven years old. I was with my mother and was visiting my sister who was studying there. I had only ever experienced the chocolate we had in Martinique: Elot, a local, quite crude chocolate, not very refined but with a pronounced cacao flavor. So we came from Martinique for a month's vacation. My sister immediately took us out to try a religieuse au chocolat (chocolate cream puff), probably knowing the shock in store for us. I had never eaten anything like it! After that moment I went out to find the best places to eat these amazing pastries, with a particular interest in mocha ones. The one at Pierre Hermé is an absolute must."

SE-CRETS OF MY

PERFECT
HOMEMADE
CHOCOLATE
CAKE

"We often inherit a taste for the beautiful and delicious things in life and in turn pass this passion on to those we love. Family recipes are a great example of this. I was brought up to be a huge fan of home-made chocolate cake, and I've since added a few touches of my own to the recipe. Here are the secrets:

CHOCOLATE
it's
physical!

"I always have lots of chocolate bars at home. Many are 90% cocoa solids because I'm really into the astringency at the moment. I feel as if chocolate is living matter, it really is physical! I especially love it when I stand on a stool and find some forgotten chocolate bars on a stack of books. These are the best kinds of discoveries!"

NEVER
LESS THEN
70 %
CHOCOLATE

66 My guilty pleasures: the Montanaro from La Maison du Chocolat and the Opéra from Lenôtre, two classic retro treats! 99

and I add a little peanut butter while decreasing the sugar. Small details that make a world of difference!"

skinnypignyc
Petrossian Caviar NYC

sandrinehuguetsicsic

#onneserefuserien

#lepurplaisir 🍫✨

nocolatmacarons 👍🏼👍🏼👍🏼🖤😆

#macaronstentation 🔶🔶

thepurevida
New York, New York

asako.627

FRANÇOIS DU CHASTEL

Founder of Chatelles

L♡VE
SLIPPERS
AND
——
CHOCOLATE!

" For women,
chocolates are like shoes:
it's all about desire, pleasure,
even addiction. They want a pair,
but then want two or three,
and eventually find any excuse
to give in to temptation. "

WHO IS *this person*
that has solved
the FEMALE *equation:* ⟶

SHOES
+ CHOCOLATE
= HAPPINESS?

At thirty years old François du Chastel left London and the world of investment banks to focus on shoes. And not just any shoes, he wanted to reinvent women's slippers in new, stylish, and creative ways. Never one to shy away from a challenge, he set out to offer fashionistas an alternative to heels and to prove that you can be hip in flats!

→ Early on he collaborated with La Maison du Chocolat to create a pair of shoes called the "Chocolate Slippers": deliciously seductive, the color of melted chocolate, and bold as brass.

They are even sold in a beautiful La Maison du Chocolat box! With this partnership he had managed to combine two of the most in-vogue women's addictions: patent leather shoes and gourmet chocolate! Well, who really acts responsibly at thirty?

Why
give
CHOCOLATES
AS A gift?

" What woman
has never said
'One
and that's it...'
just before
popping another
one,
two
or three
into their mouth? "

"MOST WOMEN
LOVE CHOCOLATE!
By giving a woman
chocolates,
you're showing her
that her happiness
is important to you.
WE ARE CONSTANTLY
ON AN ALMOST BIOLOGICAL
SEARCH
FOR PLEASURE, AND
GOURMET FOOD SATISFIES
THIS DESIRE.

WHEN EATING A CHOCOLATE
BONBON,
you feel a sense of calm
AND ENTER A PERFECTLY
INSULATED BUBBLE OF HAPPINESS.

IT'S A BEAUTIFUL
FEELING!"

Emotion N·16

NASTY

Street artist

0% COCOA CHOCOLATE

URBAN CHOC,
            is part of
        the artist's DNA,
            but for him chocolate
    is primarily a retro treat
        in the form of
            0% chocolate Milkybars.

Therefore,
    the paradox of his latest work
is that he LOVES
        CHOCOLATE
        WITHOUT CHOCOLATE !

Emotion N·17

BÉRANGÈRE LOISEAU

PR for the Bernard Loiseau Group

A
SENSORY
EXPLO-
SION

BÉRANGÈRE
TASTES, SAMPLES,
CONTEMPLATES,
INTERPRETS, TRAVELS
AND CONFIDES.

LIKE
SIPPING A FINE
VINTAGE LATE
IN THE EVENING,
FOR HER NOTHING
IS BETTER
THAN SAMPLING

SOME CHOCOLATE
BONBONS
AND REKINDLING
SOME
NOT-SO-DISTANT
MEMORIES.
HER FIRST
EXPERIENCE
WITH CHOCOLATE
WAS WHEN SHE WAS
A LITTLE GIRL

CULT URE CHOC

AND HER FATHER,
BERNARD LOISEAU,
GAVE HER
SOME CHOCOLATE
MOUSSE.

This was not a light and
airy mousse
with that sweet chocolate
little kids love,
but a dense mousse
    with dark chocolate and
        tiny air pockets.
    It was strong and rich,
        for mature palates.

This was a contest-winning
                mousse and
    the "culture choc"
    she experienced
    proved to be a baptism
of fire linto the world
        of tasting.

This initiation
    inspired her passion
for tasting, her constant
search for surprises and new
    discoveries, and for reliving
        that sensory explosion.

BÉRANGÈRE LOISEAU IS A CHOCOHOLIC.

Not just one of those who love eating it, but one of those of a rarer breed whose eyes sparkle and fingers tremble at the mere mention of chocolate. Although her palate is obviously more educated than most, she is keenly devoted to and delightfully enthusiastic about the joys of chocolate tasting, including the

STUDENT BUDGET:

RENT,
school books
AND
CHOCOLATE

V

❝ *You belong to me and all Paris belongs to me and I belong to this notebook and this pencil.* ❞

Bérangère was a student in Paris with too tight a budget to do everything the city had to offer. But Paris has an incredible concentration of chocolatiers. So she began an unusual introductory tour: chocolate tasting. But, as a demanding connoisseur, she had to set aside almost a third of her monthly budget to afford the city's best chocolates! I mean, when you have the choice between Kraft dinner or chocolates by a Meilleur Ouvrier de France, what would you choose?

illustrious events held by the famous Club des Croqueurs de Chocolat*, of which she is, of course, a member.

Write it all down!

After a childhood spent in the colorful nature of Saulieu, she found a new purpose. Alone in her Paris room, she would carefully write down her discoveries in a notebook, describing the ganaches, the textures, the luster of the chocolates she tried, and strive to put into words the fleeting sensations these treats stirred in her. Chocolate was slowly becoming a part of her daily life. It was a constant, it helped her grow, it was a reassuring presence.

11:00 a.m.?
SORRY, I CAN'T,
I HAVE AN APPOINTMENT
with
CHOCOLATE!

DRIIIING !

Late morning is when her taste buds
first feel the need for chocolate.
This realization
has prompted Bérangère Loiseau
to perform a daily ritual:
"Eleven o'clock in the morning.
This is the exact time
when I am physically and intellectually
ready for my cocoa fix.
Chocolate bonbons of course,
but also certain 'select' chocolate bars!
I make a little trip to my chocolate cache,
a personal gift from my husband,
an amazing man
who totally understands my addiction.
My chocolate cache is built
into a specially designed kitchen cabinet.
My temptations are always
for chocolate!"

* An exclusive club for chocolate enthusiasts and experts

DARK
chocolate
PIE

by La Maison du Chocolat

MAKE THE SHORTCRUST PASTRY

(makes 1 pie
for 6 people,
or 6 small pies)

- 5 oz. (140 g)
  fresh butter
- 2 oz. (60 g)
  confectioner's sugar
- 1 tablespoon (10 g)
  almond flour
- 2 pinches fine salt
- 7 oz. (200 g)
  fine flour
- 1 whole egg (50 g)
- 1/2 Tahiti vanilla pod

UTENSILS NEEDED

- One 8-inch metal pie
dish, or six 3-inch dishes
- 1 rolling pin
- 1 fine sieve or conical
strainer
- 1 bowl
- Parchment paper

Split the vanilla bean lengthwise and scrape out the seeds with the tip of a knife. Then, in a bowl, mix the butter with the vanilla seeds until it turns into a smooth cream.

Add the almond powder, salt, and sugar. Gently work the dough until it has a crumbly texture, then add the egg and sieved flour.

Knead it all together to make a smooth dough.

Then roll it out and place in the pie dish.

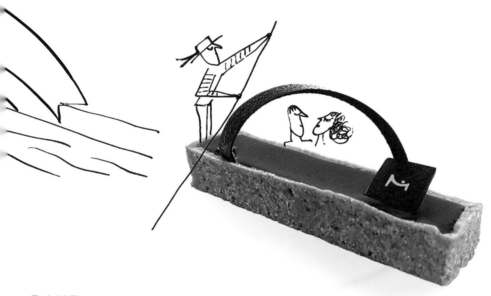

BAKE
THE PASTRY

Preheat the oven
to 300 °F. Prick the
bottom of the pastry
with a fork and place
in the oven. After 20
to 25 minutes, the pastry
should be golden brown.
Remove from the oven,
leave to cool, then
remove from the pie dish.

Pour the warm ganache
(recipe on page 119) into
the bottom of the cooked
pastry, then place the
pie in the refrigerator
for 1 hour.

MAKE
IT
LOOK
STUNNING

Randomly place
raspberries and some
little fresh mint leaves
on top of the ganache.

ANY OTHER
FINISHING
TOUCHES?

Serve the pie with
a raspberry sorbet
or sauce.

PHILIPPE LABRO

Journalist, writer, director...

I'VE   ALWAYS   LOVED

THE WORD:

chocolate!

" *Des cornichons au chocolat*
was the title of
one of my novels.
It deals with existence,
·   and finding
happiness and pleasure
among life's hardships.
I've always liked that word: 'chocolate.'
It's very evocative,
musical,
and many composers
have used it
in their lyrics.
There's a band called Hot Chocolate
and there are thousands
of songs
with chocolate in the title.
Whether you want to eat it,
drink it, look at it,
or just sing about it,
it always provides
moments
of pure pleasure. "

In a peaceful office
that seems to contain
a thousand memories,
chocolate can be found
among the vacation photos
that recall shared moments
of cradling a steaming
hot chocolate on a balcony
terrace in front of mountains.
But it is also a constant
companion and daily support
for writer Philippe Labro,
whose eyes light up
at the mention of a fine,
full-bodied grand cru
chocolate. Chocolate gives
us privileged access into the
secrets of a great man.

His childhood *was filled* —— WITH delicious COMMANDS:

"YOU'RE NOT GOING TO SCHOOL UNTIL YOU'VE FINISHED YOUR CHOCOLATE!"

This was the rule in Philippe Labro's family. And this rule was never broken. This is why chocolate is intimately linked to childhood. Chocolate is part of everyone's childhood and as common an item in the bottoms of school bags as text books themselves. It is also often the first childhood love.

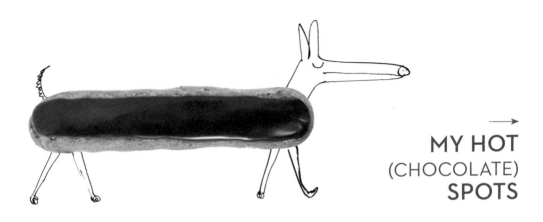

→
MY HOT
(CHOCOLATE)
SPOTS

Chocolate is comforting and an ideal fuel to combat fatigue. It is always the best way to relax, reenergize, and gain new momentum. Later on, chocolate was also one of Philippe's constant companions throughout his military service, a time when he admits to having had more than he should. The writer also admits that

"there are still two key breaks in the day —at eleven o'clock and four in the afternoon— when it is the perfect time for some chocolate."

This is when he confesses to taking out a bar of dark chocolate from his cupboard and crunching into a few squares for a pick-me-up. What do they say about never forgetting your first love?

"Café Hanselmann serves a legendary hot chocolate. Going there with my wife is a tradition when we go to St. Moritz. I love everything about it: the thickness and sweetness, and the sensation of sipping something that allows me to reconnect with the past and create a sort of delicious recurring theme. There's also a master chocolatier I have to visit, and I mean have to, when we go to Beaumont-en-Auge in Normandy: Patrick Bradfer, a connoisseur of taste, a perfectionist with an obsession for chocolate bonbons. He has proven to me that we all need rituals and one of mine is definitely to visit him and try his chocolates whenever I go to Calvados."

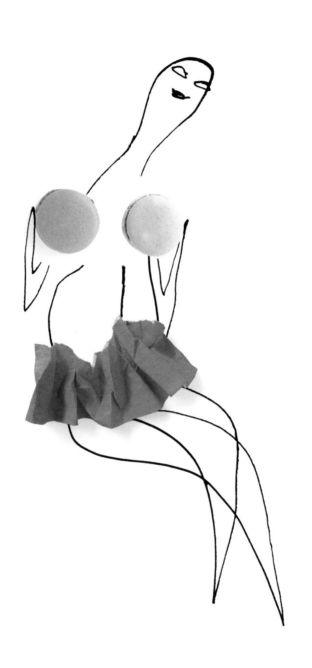

SYLVIA TOLEDANO

Jewelry designer

Gourmet

CHOC

—IN—THE—

BOX

CHOCOLATE: THE MOST CHIC TREAT YOU CAN EAT!

"To make me feel better about my gluttony, I always ensure that chocolate is part of my daily routine and that it's something amazing, inspiring, and evocative. I've always thought that it's a basic component of French luxury: it's a work of craftsmanship, sometimes packaged in signed and num-bered boxes, which surprise and delight as the lid is lifted. They are works of art of a tenth of an ounce and perfectly balanced. Chocolate provides luxury at special moments and turns a craving into something exquisite and elegant. You are more likely to be forgiven for gorging on a box of good chocolates than emptying a bag of candy."

How CHOCOLATE *saved me from* ALL-YOU-CAN-EAT BUFFETS

This jewelry designer, whose eyes light up at the mere mention of a little praline, adores chocolate and talks about it like a guilty pleasure. While she designs her creations with the same hunger as one would choose a fine restaurant, she leaves her mark on her feminine creations, colored jewels and dazzling clutch bags, with an inimitable style statement. And these small clutch bags are also her secret hiding place for guilty pleasures...

66 *I love* that feeling of *resisting* temptation and knowing that *I have* a little piece of pure pleasure *on me* at all times. 99

"I've always hated eating in public, so I have a foolproof trick:

I slip a little chocolate into my clutch, well wrapped with some tissue paper, and when I feel a little hungry, I pop it into my mouth, where it melts away with no one any the wiser.

It's a great little boost that gives me the perfect energy kick so I can mingle until late in the evening."

" There's nothing
more sensual in terms
of gourmet pleasure
than opening
a box
of chocolates.

As Oscar Wilde
once said:
'The only way
to get rid
of temptation
is to yield to it. "

Don't try to
understand,
nothing is ever as
you expect with him.

The criminal
mugshot
speaks volumes
about
his level of addiction
and is proof
of heinous chocolate
abuse.
He pleads
guilty
and admits
he is likely
to reoffend.

But when
we interrogate him
properly
and listen to
the director's cut
of his gluttony,
he makes us
immediately start
scribbling in our
notebooks
and gives us
privileged access
to his dark
(chocolate) world.

If you've
never met
a real chocoholic,
James Huth is the
archetypal person
who not only
loves chocolate
but makes you
want to eat it too.

Emotion N. 20

JAMES HUTH

Director of *Brice de Nice* (among others)

ANATOMY
of a Chocoholic

- [ ] Tu préfères le chocolat à la vanille.
- [ ] Tu ne peux pas offrir une boîte de chocolats sans en acheter pour to
- [ ] Tu as déjà vidé un pot de glace au chocolat de 500 ml devant la té
- [ ] Tu mets de la sauce chocolat en plus de la boule de glace.
- [ ] Tu es capable de parcourir plus de 10 kms pour trouver du chocola
- [ ] Tu rajoutes toujours des copeaux sur ta mousse au chocolat.
- [ ] Tu ne peux pas manger un rocher sans en manger deux.
- [ ] Tu préfères la pâte crue chocolatée au gâteau cuit.
- [ ] Tu repères immédiatement les desserts au chocolat sur un menu.
- [ ] Tu ne vas à l'hôtel que pour les chocolats sur l'oreiller.
- [ ] Tu peux tuer sans ta dose journalière de chocolat.
- [ ] Tu te moques de la surprise dans le Kinder.

Si vous avez deux croix ou plus dans cette liste, il est fortemen
conseillé de consulter rapidement le chocolatier le plus proche

THE CULPRIT HAS A NAME

Travel
Essen-
tials

*"Chocolate
is so magical
that even the word
brings on
a craving.
And then
you just have
to head straight out
to the
chocolate shop!"*

"I shot *Brice de Nice 3* on a beach in Thailand. We left with the team for seven weeks. Of course, we had to fill up with chocolate before we left because you never know whether you'll find any when you get there! We ended up eight pounds over our baggage limit because of all the chocolate bars, pralines, marzipans, and other chocolate candy we had to take with us. But who's counting?"

"My chocolate of choice? Rochers, dark or milk. I love that incredible sensation of crunching through the outer layer to the soft center, which then melts in your mouth. And my guilty pleasure: chocolate marzipans, usually with dark chocolate. When the balance is just right, it's amazing! The Jolika by La Maison du Chocolat is one of those chocolates I eat compulsively."

"Just very recently, I crossed to the other side of Paris to find Arnaud Larher's chocolate cake, which I had discovered at a friend's house the day before. And I'm prone to go out to buy a few bars and come back with more than 6 pounds of different chocolates for a family tasting session!"

HOW HOOKED ARE YOU?

Translation : Page 191

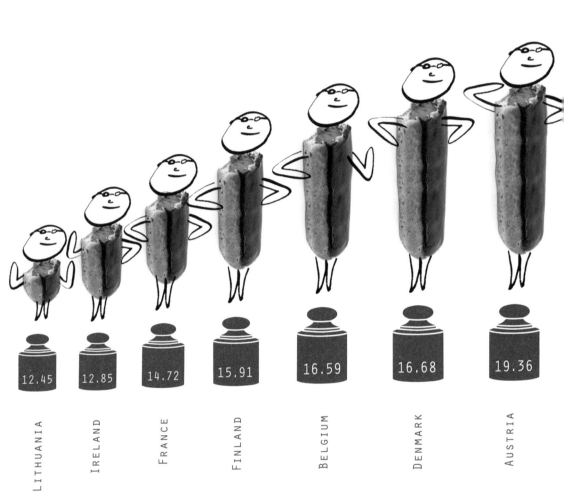

LITHUANIA 12.45

IRELAND 12.85

FRANCE 14.72

FINLAND 15.91

BELGIUM 16.59

DENMARK 16.68

AUSTRIA 19.36

THE TOP 10 BIGGEST

19.49

25.74

26.88 POUNDS

UNITED KINGDOM

SWITZERLAND

GERMANY

CHOCOLATE CONSUMERS **IN EUROPE**

PER YEAR
IN POUNDS
PER CAPITA

CHOCOLATE

DARK

as the night

TONINO BENACQUISTA

Writer

For those who want to know
the secret for what inspires great writers,
it's this: explore
your life experiences.
The sensitivity of youth
is often fertile ground for unique
and evocative stories.
And when such a story
centers on chocolate,   it can lead
to a charmingly
poetic recollection.

ALL ABOARD
THE CHOCOLATE
EXPRESS

Passions often stem from a single memory. Although chocolate has never been an object of fantasy for Tonino Benacquista, it is still one of the protagonists of a happy memory of his younger life.

When he was twenty-two years old, the aspiring writer had not yet attracted interest from a publish-ing house. He wanted to become an author, but making a living from it proved to be a challenge. Writing needs time, lots of it, and constant attention.

To make ends meet, he decided to join the Compagnie Internationale des grands express européens (International European Great Expresses Company), working on the Paris to Rome line.
On these trips, Tonino would look after about sixty passengers. He would give out sheets and blan-kets, and then take their tickets and passports so he wouldn't have to wake them up when going through customs in Switzerland and Italy.

This is when chocolate surprisingly enters the scene.

"At about half past one in the morning, our train, the Galileo, would stop at the border crossing of Vallorbe in Switzerland. This is when you show the identity papers of the passengers who are sleep-ing soundly. After this, there was not a lot left to do until we arrived in Venice. So we would spend twenty minutes or so at the station in Vallorbe.

On the platform, there was always an old man with a white cart who would ring a small bell to attract the attention of night owls like us. Each time, he would almost wake up our guests by waving his bell, the noise of which was always ten times louder in the silence of the station. So we would rush over to him and buy some chocolate from him so he would stop ringing the bell.

He sold praline bites and Swiss chocolates, of course. Like everyone else, I would stock up on chocolates on this wet station platform and then enjoy them alone in my compartment.

This chocolate ritual would be a rare moment of peace and quiet for me. The chocolate would melt slowly in my mouth, wake up my taste buds and symbolize the start of my quiet night, bringing me reassurance that now the sleeping passengers would not wake until Venice.

This chocolate represented a time for calm, a moment for me and me alone.

From this and other fascinating experiences on the Grands Express européens, a book was born: *La Maldonne des sleepings*. Furthermore, from this was also born a lifelong love of chocolate, dark as the night."

Emotion N. 22

LAURE HÉRIARD-DUBREUIL

Founder of the boutique The Webster, United States

CHOCOLATE
it's
ecstasy!

The stores founded by Laure Hériard-Dubreuil have become iconic for Americans looking for the ultimate in French style. Laure integrates any piece of luxury she can into her daily life with natural ease and impeccable taste. Among her daily essentials, chocolate seems to be a little piece of France that she cannot and would not give up.

CHOCOLATE:
a clean break
BE-
FORE
MOVING ON!

"The first word that comes to mind when talking about chocolate is ecstasy! It sounds like a big word for such a small thing, but it sums up all of the emotions I feel when eating it. Pleasure,

——→

EVERYONE
has
CHOCOLATE
memories

"We all have chocolate memories: a photo of children with ice cream or pastry cream smeared all around their mouths, spoons scraping every last drop of a mixing bowl, punishments for finishing all the Easter chocolates that should have been shared. ——→

→

excitement, desire... It is true what they often say about patience being a virtue and absence making the heart grow fonder, but none of that applies for me and chocolate. I crack, and it feels so good! It's a genuine moment of pleasure for yourself. For me it's usually in the evening, after dinner, when I can sit down with some chocolate and unwind after my day's work. It's an important step: to break off a few squares, enjoy, and then move on to something else!"

THE FINE COLLECTIONS OF CHOCOLATE AND FASHION

"I find it amazing that anything can be made from chocolate: from the simplest, most subtle shape, to the purest and most complex creation. We can create small squares on chocolate bars, delicate hand-made truffles, or real works of art: dresses, objects, characters, and much more. We see a lot of these during Easter in the fine chocolate shops. The world of chocolate is a large one to explore, just like fashion. We can dream and be as creative as we want, with unlimited possibilities."

→

My grandmother's hot chocolate, so thick that a spoon could stand in it. The chocolatey kisses of my two-year-old son who always wants more. Chocolate is all about these little moments of laughter, smiling, and happiness— snapshots of family life that we want to revisit time and time again."

Among the jobs
everyone would love to have,
that of Jacques Pessis would
be right up there. The President
of the Club des Croqueurs de
Chocolat* has privileged access
to the greatest chocolate artisans,
including many that have become
famous thanks to the expertise
of his club members.
On his favorite subject, he paints
an appetizing picture of artists and
artisans from this highly prized world,
a world full of emotions and memories
and wonderful chocolatey flavor.
And this club seems to have been
formed from nothing more than
a simple gathering of addicts
finally admitting their weakness
to one another!

* An exclusive club for chocolate
  enthusiasts and experts

JACQUES PESSIS

Journalist and President
of the Club des Croqueurs de Chocolat

Chocoholics ANO-NYMOUS

The CHOCO-HOLICS

Le Club des Croqueurs de Chocolat was founded around a dinner table one evening. Each of the friends there happened to order the same dessert: the famous Pleyel, a chocolate cake by legendary chocolatier Robert Linxe, founder of La Maison du Chocolat. Claude Lebey put forward the idea of creating a club for chocolate enthusiasts, to find the best artisans in the business and to celebrate the exquisite creations they make. The club's members are a group of one hundred and fifty handpicked experts who take part in blind chocolate tastings and note down their appraisals in a little guide the size of a chocolate bar. Essential reading!

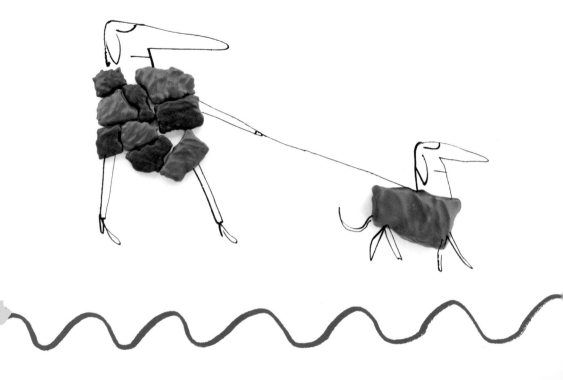

JAPAN is also MAD ABOUT CHOCOLATE !

CHOCOLATE SPREAD

↓

"There was only one chocolate boutique in France in 1977: La Maison du Chocolat. But there are now more than forty thousand chocolatiers around the country."

"For Japanese tourists, a trip to France must include three stops: the Moulin Rouge, the Eiffel Tower, and a chocolate boutique. WHO WOULD HAVE THOUGHT CHOCOLATE WOULD FOLLOW IN THE FOOTSTEPS OF THESE TWO FRENCH ICONS?

Japan's interest in chefs is still as strong as ever and the great chocolate brands there all have French names. Western traditions can be popular with the Japanese: one of the major festivals celebrated there is Valentine's Day, when it is not uncommon to queue for more than six hours outside a chocolate shop waiting to be served!"

FLORENCE CATHIARD

Owner of
Château Smith Haut Lafitte

A TALE *of* Two GRAND CRUS

Although Florence Cathiard is primarily known for fine vintages from her Smith Haut Lafitte vineyard, she is still very attached to another kind of grand cru—that of the chocolate kind from France's leading chocolatiers. Having found similarities between wine and chocolate and realizing

Terroir and the same emotions

how essential this was to their enjoyment, she created a tasting tour to pair the two for visitors of her Bordeaux vineyard.

"I'm a big fan of chocolate and I had to find a way to incorporate chocolate into the tours we offer to wine enthusiasts visiting our vineyard. Analyzing the sensations that chocolate induces when visiting a château like Smith Haut Lafitte may seem somewhat unusual, but it's not at all! They both have the concept of terroir in common, ⟶

Traveling *the — world — with* CHOCOLATE

"Both wine and chocolate take us on a voyage. Wine is a time machine that takes us back to landscapes, sun-soaked hillsides, and valleys that were blessed with a unique amount of sunshine in any given year. As for chocolate, it takes you on a journey through incredible countries, many of which will never have been visited by food lovers, but which still manage to evoke hundreds of images through the flavor of their products. To taste, savor, and feel, is to travel! That's why I wanted people to be able to discover our wines through

landscapes evoked by chocolate: to offer wine from young vines with a 70% Peruvian chocolate so the spicy notes, caramel, and sweet vanilla can be discovered; to depict the Smith hills with a more full-bodied choco-late that grabs one's attention immediately. It's absolutely magical when you start to understand the associations between wines and other fine foods, to build bridges, to bring together worlds that superficially seem so far apart. Chocolate and wine is like a successful marriage that continues to surprise!"

" Incorporating
chocolate
into wine
discovery
is a great reason
to always
have it around! "

WE LEARN
SO MUCH FROM
ENJOYING
A GRAND CRU!

———→

which generates very
special emotions related
to growing and nature. In
both industries, we are
permanently connected to
nature and how our crops
grow. We are at their mercy.
This simple fact creates
an emotion in itself, when
several months or years
after harvest, be it grapes
or cacao pods, we test
our crea-tions. We sample
the result of the work of a
whole chain of dedicated
professionals."

"It's easy to see the relationship
between chocolate and wine when
we realize that both use the label
'grand cru,' a term reserved for the finest
foods. These two worlds spin side by side,
offering up the ultimate in gustatory
pleasure. This is always the emotion
you seek to provoke:

TO CREATE
SOMETHING UNIQUE,
A SENSORY EXPERIENCE
THAT BECOMES
A TRUE LIFE EXPERIENCE.

Wine traces our footprints
and chocolate records the terroirs
that have contributed to its history
and delicacy we know today.
It is an emotional story, history
in the making. Wine and chocolate
tell the story of their country
of origin better than a teacher can."

seiko_fujii
Roppongi Hills

#unevilleacroquer 🤫🖤👗💅

MAXIME HOERTH

Best Craftsman of France, Head Barman at Le Bristol Paris

CHALLENGE ACCEPTED!

With chocolate and cocktails, it's like speed dating: you only have a few minutes, or even seconds to captivate someone. After confessing that he likes "all kinds of chocolate," Maxime Hoerth, a Meilleur Ouvrier de France (master craftsman) and Head Barman of Le Bristol Paris, recounts his reaction when La Maison du Chocolat asked him to design cocktails that would pair well with chocolate; but they had to be alcohol free!

An unfair CHALLENGE

66 How can you ask someone
to make a cocktail without
alcohol? It's like asking
Nicolas Cloiseau

to come up
with a recipe for
a chocolate without
using cocoa! But because
I love challenges, I was
tempted to take this one on.
So I worked with Nicolas,
and together we found complementary
flavors and worked on pairings until
we had found the right chemistry. 99

The ART *of* —— MIXOLOGY

66 The cocktail world has so many
parallels with the chocolate
world that we quickly understood
what we had to do. We are in the
business of sharing and pleasure.
What we do is make people
happy by introducing them to new
sensations and new flavors.

And when you're lucky to have a job
that involves sharing your passion,
it's hard to beat! To design a cocktail
without alcohol, I had to rethink my job
and get back to basics, and that proved
to be an incredible challenge. But we
did it, and the result is very pleasing. 99

Faubourg COCKTAIL

by **Maxime Hoerth**

Here's the secret recipe for the Faubourg cocktail.
This one is with alcohol and goes perfectly with dark ganache truffles.
It's a short drink cocktail, shaken and served in a "coupette" glass.

INGREDIENTS

- 2 oz. vodka infused with bourbon vanilla
- 2/3 oz. lime juice
- 2/3 oz. "mille-fleurs" honey syrup
- 1 1/3 oz. passion fruit purée
- 1/3 oz. fresh mango purée

Fill a cocktail shaker two-thirds full with ice.

Pour all the ingredients into the shaker.
Put the lid on the shaker and shake for thirty seconds.

Using a fine mesh sieve, double strain the mixture into a cocktail glass that has been pre-chilled in the freezer.

Add half a passion fruit for garnish.

CHOCOLATE Ganache

Recipe by **La Maison du Chocolat**

What's this for? Use this ganache to fill or top cakes.
It's also great for eating by the spoonful, but you'll need
to do it quickly before greedy family members pounce on the bowl!
Tip: Make sure no one else is around or knows what you're doing
if you actually want to finish making your ganache!

SHOPPING LIST

- 7 oz. (200 ml) fresh cream
- 7 oz. (200 g) dark chocolate (60% cocoa solids)
- 1 oz. (25 g) fresh butter

UTENSILS NEEDED

- 1 spatula
- 1 whisk
- 1 bowl
- 1 saucepan

METHOD

1

Chop the chocolate into small pieces and set aside in a bowl.

2

In a saucepan, bring the cream to a boil, then pour over the chocolate, covering it completely.

3

Leave the chocolate to melt for 2 minutes without mixing, then use a whisk to gently stir the mixture in small circles from the center to the outside.

4

When the ganache thickens, make larger circles toward the outside to obtain a really smooth texture.

5

Then add the butter in small pieces and mix to create a velvety ganache.

ALICE ET JÉRÔME TOURBIER

Founders of Les Sources de Caudalie
and Les Étangs de Corot

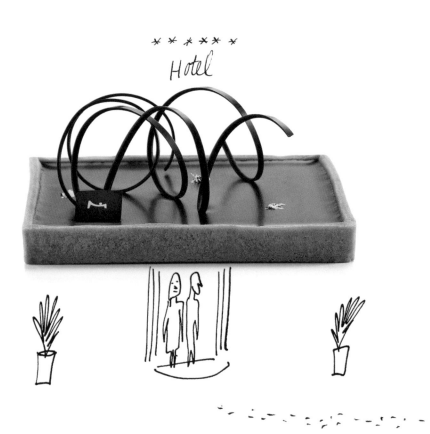

We can share everything in life,
including success, but this doesn't
mean tastes and colors (of chocolate)
need to be the same.
Alice and Jérôme Tourbier have
big ideas that work, especially those
involving vineyard hotels.
But when it comes to chocolate,
they do not always agree
and fiercely stand
their ground.

FACE TO ƎƆAℲ
WITH CHOCOLATE

We pose some tricky
questions and receive
some strong opinions back
from two foodies who know
what they like. Here is the
evidence that good food
is an essential part of
the Tourbier household!

DOUBLE CHO C OLATE

Alice

Jérôme

WHAT CHOCOLATE DO YOU LOVE?

I love very dark chocolate, almost astringent, the type where you look at the cocoa percentage before anything else. I always have a bar of 75% Swiss chocolate with me. I try to resist, but I always end up giving in to temptation.

There's certainly not just one type of chocolate I like. I love several types. I regularly have to exercise self-restraint. Chocolate is my only addiction, the only compulsive purchase I make. I have a real weakness for the signature dessert of our chef Nicolas Masse: a chocolate and Noisettine de Médoc cake. It's incredible and leaves me speechless every time. It's the kind of cake you don't want to touch because it's so pretty, but once you tuck in, you can't stop. It's crunchy, it melts, it fills your mouth with pure deliciousness... it's amazing.

DO YOU HAVE ANY CHOCOLATE MEMORIES?

A delicious snack every day at half past four when I got home from school. I was (already) very greedy when I was young. I would eat some good bread and two bars of milk chocolate. And, of course, I ate the chocolate before the bread!

Chocolate always brings back happy memories. For me, it's the hot chocolate my grandmother made me with real pieces of milk chocolate. It was served by my grandfather who was a waiter at the Café de Flore in Paris. It's my equivalent memory to Proust's madeleine cakes

WHAT CHOCOLATE IS IN A CATEGORY OF ITS OWN?

The cocoa-coffee crumble from the chef of Les Étangs de Corot, or the chocolate macaroons from Carette on Place de Trocadéro in Paris. You have to try them!

The chocolate tart with Eure saffron made by our chef, and how something so simple is taken to a whole new level. I particularly like it when contrasts are striking, when you integrate something subtle into a classic dessert.

The chocolate spread I make for the whole family: guaranteed palm oil free, rich, creamy, smooth, and perfect for gorging yourself on an empty stomach!

WHAT IS YOUR "HOMEMADE" CHOCOLATE?

◄──────── ────────►

Under-cooked chocolate birthday cakes. Even if it goes wrong or the proportions are not quite right, we do it as a family and that's half the charm. Chocolate is often associated with celebrations and happy times.

Definitely mornings, to make sure the day gets off to a good start. Chocolate is a fantastic booster!

WHEN IS YOUR "CHOCOLATE TIME"?

◄──────── ────────►

Evenings, it goes hand in hand with relaxation. For those of us who work with food, we have to be very disciplined. You can't let yourself indulge too much, just a little treat every now and again. Chocolate has replaced our dessert, so we have a bit of chocolate to finish our glass of wine.

WHAT CHOCOLATE DO YOU LIKE TO SHARE?

────────►

Bars of chocolate with the kids. I've replaced all the candy bars with proper artisan chocolate. It's a way of educating young palates while enjoying a little indulgence!

│
▼

Birthday chocolate cake!

AND WHAT DO YOU NOT LIKE TO SHARE?

I hate sharing my chocolate dessert. Every bite is mine, all mine!

My dark chocolate. It suits me that my children prefer milk chocolate!

◄──────── ────────►

White chocolate. ◄──── WHAT CHOCOLATE DO YOU NEVER TOUCH? ────► White chocolate.

French

English

Slovak

Spanish

Russian

HANA LÊ VAN

Fashion photographer
@journeyintolavillelumiere Instagrammer

THE LANGUAGE OF CHOCOLATE IS UNIVERSAL

Hana is young, but has still managed to live in six different countries already and speaks five languages fluently. She left her native Slovakia to live with her French husband she met in Australia and now resides in Paris where her ongoing mission is to unearth the latest in Parisian style. Wherever she goes she is accompanied by tens of thousands of Instagram followers, who watch her exploits closely and often find themselves tempted by delicious images of chocolate!

Tempting *her* FOLLOWERS

"I like to think that my Instagram photos make people want to get out, eat, sit down in a café, discover a chocolate soufflé, walk through the Tuileries Garden and enjoy a Cédric Gino pastry at Le Meurice. I like to think that gourmet images provide gourmet pleasure themselves!"

MAGIC
↓
BOX
↑
CHOCO

"My Magic Box is a secret box I safeguard at home containing all sorts of gifts that I like to give to people whenever I want. It's filled with French luxury brands, little works of art, pretty objects and, of course, chocolates. The chocolates are from La Maison du Chocolat because they're examples of how amazing French food can be."

— #fanforever

"We don't have this culture of pastry and chocolates in Slovakia, although we do love good food. My mother was an amazing cook, my father owned a restaurant and my sister is now a chef in Austria! So it's no surprise that I like to keep abreast of everything delicious. My arrival in France was the start of a lifelong love affair I was to have with the exquisite food from our top chefs, such as Pierre Marcolini, Nicolas Cloiseau and Cédric Grolet."

“ My time for chocolate
is in the evening,
after dinner. ”

ALAIN PASSARD

Head Chef at the three-Michelin-starred restaurant L'Arpège

CHEF'S
SPECIAL

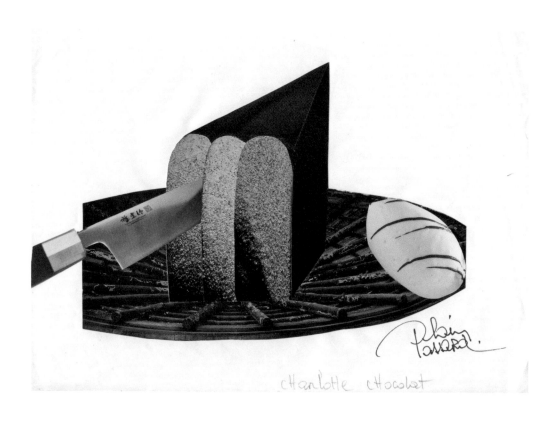

Charlotte chocolat

CHOCOLATE
ALWAYS
OFFERS
A PLATFORM
FOR CREATIVITY,

AND NOT
JUST IN A
CULINARY
SENSE.

Alain Passard loves vegetables, but also colors and delicate pairings that are as much a feast for the eyes as for the mouth. His creative dishes surprise and delight every time. Although he seems to be never short of ideas for innovative dishes, chocolate provides him with a new playground for letting his imagination run free.

ALAIN PASSARD

From warm brown
folded paper and silk
thread, to a small bag with
an iconic logo: all provide
a creative outlet for self-
expression. With folds,
weaves, stitches and white
chalk, Alain Passard finds
a way to express the
emotion of chocolate and
love of cocoa in his own
inimitable way.

"Mille-feuilles (1000 leaves) for takeout"

lostncheeseland
La Maison du Chocolat

#lovedanceandchocolate 😊😊

grace_ann_pierce

davidarcamone
Piazza San marco - Venezia

#sodelicatesochocolate 😜 🍫   #pasvupaspris 🍫 🐺 🤍 🤍 🤍 🖤

 jo_bazaar

#lechocolatpourtous 🐺

GILLES DESCÔTES

Chef de Cave (cellar master) at Champagne Bollinger

Gilles Descôtes
holds the
highly prestigious post
of Chef de cave
at Bollinger,

the renowned Champagne house. It goes without saying, therefore, that he knows all about aroma, flavor notes, and the subtleties of excellent taste. For Gilles, chocolate used to be a treat to indulge in from time to time when he found a particular chocolate bar he liked. But all that changed when he found himself at a specialized tasting...

← THE —

(COCOA)

FAT

OF THE

LAND →

"A Danish winemaker friend of mine once invited me to take part in a chocolate tasting. It was rather a unusual invitation for me because, as a chef de cave of a Champagne house, I'm not often approached by chocolate makers. Champagne and chocolate are not known for going together well because the sugar in chocolate brings out the acidity in champagne. But I was willing to give it a go and decided to try something new. The chocolate and wine were a bold pairing and I was finding it difficult to use my

knowledge of champagne to do this tasting successfully. I was clearly struggling to find a common thread. But gradually, over the course of the tasting, I discovered what champagne and chocolate had

THAT
won't
WORK!
...
Although
...

→

in common: the notion
of terroir, of belonging to
a region, a country, a particular
type of land. The two products
seemed to be united by this
idea of the land, as well as by
the desire to express an idea
through a product. One asks
us to describe its color, its body,
its character, while the other
wants us to contemplate the
origin of the beans, how they
have been roasted,
the associations, the textures.
This was when I understood
chocolate's finesse,
its variations, its rough
edges and, essentially,
its immense richness."

"But there is a big 'but.' The
marriage of chocolate and
champagne is a risky one! You
really don't want to let them get
on the wrong side of each other.
With champagne's acidity and
chocolate's sweetness—*wham!*—
you lose all the subtle delicacy of
champagne. However, that hasn't
stopped chocolate enthusiasts
from experimenting and seeking
new discoveries. Some bold and
expert establishments, such as
La Maison du Chocolat, have
created some sublime pairings
with a ganache dipped in melted
chocolate and then plunged
into champagne! A challenge
successfully beaten and a pure
delight!"

IT NEEDS
TO CRUNCH!

"I'm one of those who likes to find things in chocolate. I love the feeling of chocolate gently melting in the mouth, and then suddenly crunching a hazelnut, an almond, or a raisin or nougat. I love it when the ingredients and textures come together and create their own harmonies. I love the combination of flavors with roasted nuts. And I will happily pair it with a ten-year-old champagne. When you love something, you indulge!"

May I
suggest…

"One of my tasks as chef de cave is to provide inspiration for chefs so they can pair great foods. To those who can't say no to an irresistible chocolate dessert, I suggest a black forest with cherries, which has the same pinot noir notes found in champagne. I can say with some certainty that this will be fantastic!"

ARMEN PETROSSIAN

CEO of Petrossian

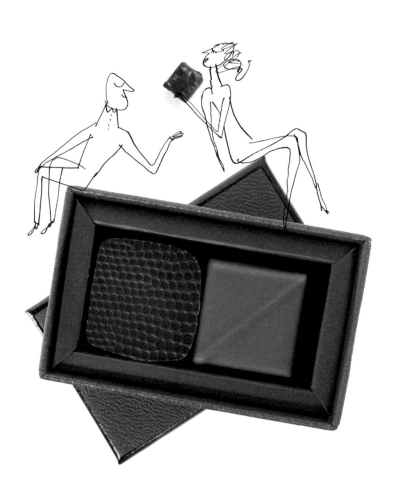

ONE MORE?
YES
PLEASE!

The best
farmed caviar:
check!

Delicious vodka
to accompany this
sturgeon roe at any
time of the year:
check!

And polished
chocolates like
sparkling pearls:
check!

The biggest
name in caviar:
check!

ARMEN PETROSSIAN

expertly continues the traditions
of a family that first captured the hearts
and palates of the French nearly one hundred
years ago. And while caviar made the Petrossian
name famous, its range of gourmet chocolates
is simply adding to its renown.

The best gifts are the ones you want to keep for yourself

" When I think of chocolate, I always remember this one memorable dinner my wife and I were invited to. As we often did, we decided to bring a big box of our favorite chocolates from La Maison du Chocolat. We arrived at our hosts and were treated to a wonderful evening. After dinner, our friend served coffee and opened the box of chocolates we had brought. They were offered around, we gladly accepted, and they were delicious. One more?

Yes please! But, out of politeness, we couldn't accept any more. It was a difficult decision and we were disappointed not to be able to continue sampling these little treasures. My wife and I exchanged looks. BUT THE VERY NEXT DAY, WE WENT STRAIGHT BACK TO THE SHOP TO GET TWO POUNDS OF CHOCOLATE EACH. WE THEN PROCEEDED TO POLISH THEM ALL OFF THAT VERY WEEKEND! "

WHY NOT MILK CHOCO- LATE?

" I noticed that whenever I ask a friend: 'What kind of chocolate do you prefer?', he responds: 'dark chocolate,' but WHENEVER I OPEN A BOX OF CHOCOLATES, THE FIRST TO BE GRABBED ARE THE MILK CHOCOLATES. Go figure! "

COMMONALITIES
between

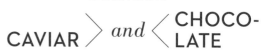

CAVIAR ⟩ *and* ⟨ CHOCO- LATE

They make you happy!

They elicit great moods.

They have an energizing effect.

They provide moments of pure pleasure.

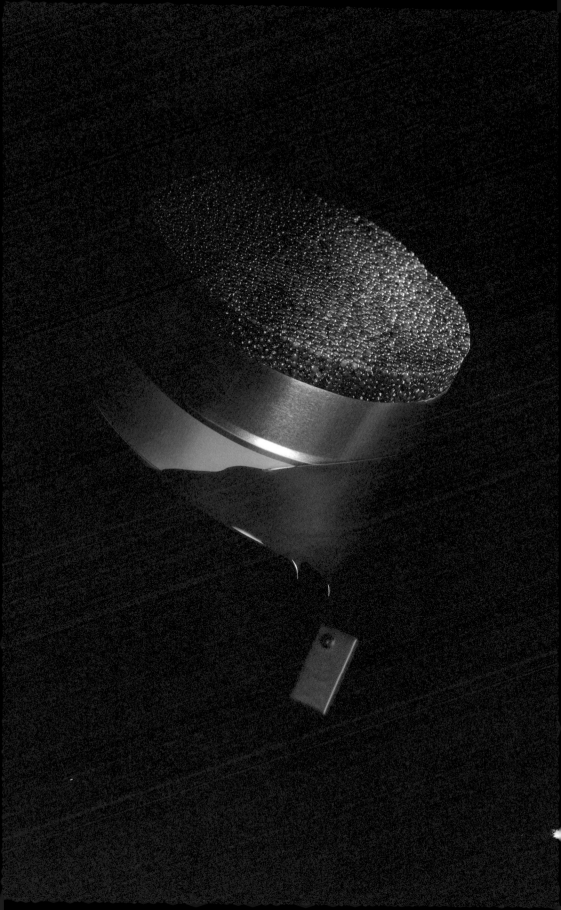

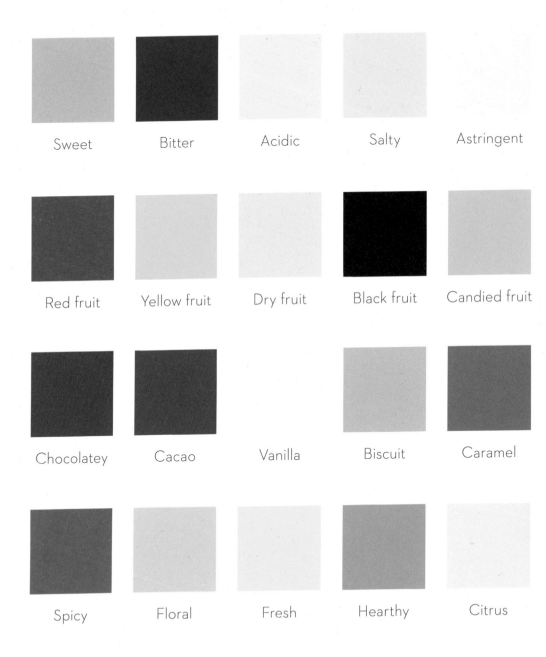

Sweet	Bitter	Acidic	Salty	Astringent
Red fruit	Yellow fruit	Dry fruit	Black fruit	Candied fruit
Chocolatey	Cacao	Vanilla	Biscuit	Caramel
Spicy	Floral	Fresh	Hearthy	Citrus

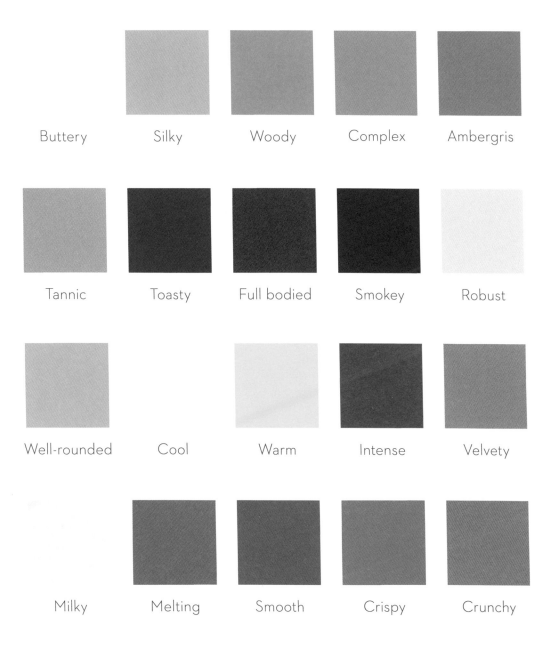

Buttery	Silky	Woody	Complex	Ambergris
Tannic	Toasty	Full bodied	Smokey	Robust
Well-rounded	Cool	Warm	Intense	Velvety
Milky	Melting	Smooth	Crispy	Crunchy

Emotion N. 31

SARAH LAVOINE

Interior Designer and Architect

WHO ———— WOULD BELIEVE YOU HIDE

———————

CHOCOLATE?

Chocolate is a very personal
religion. Sarah Lavoine made her
choice a long time ago and she fully accepts it.
The young interior designer makes no bones
about her love for chocolate, a subject
many feel is impolite to broach.
But you never forget young love,
which is why memories of her consuming passion
for crunchy chocolate come flooding back...

Are you born
ADDICTED
or
do you
become
ADDICTED
?

She starts off by claiming

"I'm not addicted to chocolate, although..."

before proceeding to lose herself in memories of Crunch bars that literally crunched before melting in the mouth (and on fingers) and of whole bars gobbled up to overcome a cigarette craving (because there's nothing like experiencing bliss to recover →

CACAO
—
CACHE

"Chocolate is like falling for someone. When you find a chocolate you love, you can't stop thinking about it. In just a few weeks, it becomes an essential food in your kitchen cabinet (placed very high so children can't reach it), or even in your bedroom (who would believe you hide chocolate!). Chocolate often provides moments of pure joy, like when you think to yourself 'I want some' and then you realize you have some! You have this little rush of excitement knowing that any minute now you'll be able to wonderfully satisfy your intense craving."

Addict TACTIC

"I love chocolate caramels because caramel is always linked to happy memories of childhood greed. I always look for them when I'm handed a box of chocolates, and because it's polite to take the first one you reach for rather than spend time choosing, I've learned to recognize the chocolate caramels of certain chocolatiers."

→ from nasty addictions).
"I console myself by saying that not all addictions are equally bad and that there are worse evils than succumbing to these red, white, and blue bars, which, for better or worse, are now sold in threes! And as the French saying goes: 'Where there is discomfort, there is no pleasure.' I can and do live by this philosophy!"

OLIVIER CRESP

Master perfumer

A DELICIOUS CHOCOLATEY AROMA

Olivier Cresp is one of those
rare and exceptional people
who have the ability to identify
and make sense of
all the smells that surround us.
In a world of thousands of aromas,
chocolate was one of the scents
that came to inspire the unusual work
conducted between
Olivier and Nicolas Cloiseau
of La Maison du Chocolat
as they joined forces
to explore the sensory links
between fragrances and chocolate.

A NEW
SCENT FAMILY
for food lovers!

"Creating a perfume is primarily about consulting a library of fragrances you've built up over time. Mine has always included childhood memories: granny smith apples, pralines, caramelized candy apples... All these recollections led me to create a scent family for food lovers! $\longrightarrow$

It's hard to imagine to what extent our sources
of inspirations are intimately linked to
unforgettable moments in our lives. The memories
and images that shape Olivier Cresp's inspiration
have a mistery and power that only he can interpret
and ultimately use for his very personal and
very universal creations.

→ When Nicolas Cloiseau asked me to work with him on new chocolate aromas, I knew we were going to ex-plore a common area: one of love for food, a mouthwatering world in which the senses go wild. How could we depict the smell of the sea, of summer air, and hot chocolate? The goal was to reinterpret the emotional connection to our childhood in order to offer a modern vision of sensory discovery. Although we didn't use the same tools, our exploration and goals were similar: the search for the perfect combination, for ideal bal-ance, for the respect we have for the past and for boldness. Enjoying a chocolate bonbon is just like smelling a perfume: they are both about recollecting and discovering."

FLEETING
—— *pleasures*

"The challenge for me was that I could only work with a few dozen possible combinations, whereas I normally have over twelve hundred raw materials in my perfumery, in addition to three thousand synthetic molecules. And I had to see how chocolate worked its magic in the briefest of pleasurable moments. Where-as perfume lasts on the skin for a while,

CHOCOLATE ONLY HAS
A FEW SECONDS TO MELT
IN THE MOUTH AND DELIVER
ITS UNIQUE EXPERIENCE.

This is what I was looking for and tried to capture: the magic of a flee-ting pleasure."

OLIVIER CRESP

Awake-
ning

Creating and tasting
chocolate both incite
special emotions:

*they
evoke
images*

the

*they
awaken
sensations*

*they
stimulate
desire and
emotion*

Senses

KÉTHÉVANE DAVRICHEWY

Writer

I like to indulge....

DELIC
FOOD
THO

I need my fix of chocolate every day!

I'm crazy about chocolate bonbons....

I love dark chocolate...

IOUS
FOR
UGHT!

I really like milk chocolate...

I adore pralines...

"I don't know why,
but eating chocolate
helps me to write
assertively and with
real authenticity. It's like
deliciously inspiring food
for thought. I feel like
my taste buds and brain
are directly connected.
But while the pure
pleasure of chocolate
puts me into a state of
Zen and calms me down,
I also feel intense anxiety
when the box is empty.
This provides me with
a necessary break,
just enough time to
go out and stock up!"

FROM *modest*
CONFESSION
—*to*—
FULL-BLOWN
ADMISSION
OF GUILT!

"Chocolate has always
been part of my reading
ritual. I can barely savor the
lines I'm reading with-out
a few ounces of chocolate.
Reading is like a date with
yourself, one you arrange
every day to discover new
worlds. It's funny to think
that my joy of reading is
intimately linked to my ⟶

Right in the heart of the 6th
arrondissement, between the
Saint-Sulpice church and
Saint-Germain-des-Prés
square, is the office
of Kéthévane Davrichewy.

Such a setting provides
the perfect inspiration for
a writer at work. The famous
bars and cafés of the area leap
straight into her imagination
and onto the pages of her

DEEP DARK CHOCOLATE SECRET

little chocolate ritual. I find a comfy chair and always prepare a small spread of everything I love: a nice tea, praline chocolates... It's like a date with sweetness I allow myself in that moment. One more? Why not!"

"I once had the idea of organizing a private chocolate tasting at home for my husband, who is a big chocolate fan. I walked around the whole district, seeking out the best chocolatiers, excited about the taste sensations in store for him (and for me as well, of course). While I was trying to choose my chocolates in one of the nice stores I had discovered a few blocks from our house, the salesper-son tried to help me by asking me what kind of chocolate my husband liked. I tried to paint a pic-ture of my husband and his likes, and I can't remember which detail it was, but he suddenly ex-claimed, 'Ah, I know! It's the gentleman who comes in every morning for his rocher!' Proof that there are many dirty secrets in-volving chocolate!"

novels. An inveterate foodie who regularly strolls the streets of Paris looking for her next cocoa fix, she speaks of chocolate as if admitting a secret weakness.

Emotion N. 34

CARRIE SOLOMON

Photographer

UNLIMITED

CHOCOLATE

Carrie Solomon
is a young American
photographer who has
lived in Paris for the last
ten years. As well as raising
two gorgeous little girls,
she writes mouthwatering
books about food. But she
is also a fan of chocolate
in all its forms, especially
those that reconnect her
with the United States.

A Yule log in August? Why not!

"When you are a photographer, there are moments when you feel the world is spinning off axis. This is what I felt when I found myself photographing a famous pastry chef's Yule log in the middle of August. I thought such a treat was the ultimate reward for a hard day of shooting (well, you can't really throw something like that in the trash!). I volunteered to 'dispose' of it because no one else seemed interested. Real luxury is precisely this kind of unexpected pleasure, to experience what no one else can and to enjoy these unique little moments. That's why I pounced on the Yule log with a fork once the shoot had ended... only to find it was made of plaster!"

Your job must be HARD!

"TO BE ABLE TO WORK WITH CHOCOLATIERS IS VERY LUCKY. I MADE A BOOK ON TWENTY-FIVE PASTRY CHEFS AND CHOCOLATIERS AND I WOULD REGULARLY COME HOME LADEN WITH CHOCOLATE MACAROONS, COCONUT CAKE, TRUFFLES, AND OTHER CHOCOLATE BONBONS. NOW, I'M PRETTY GREEDY, BUT IT WAS TOO MUCH, EVEN FOR ME. SO I WOULD TAKE A SMALL GOURMET PACKAGE TO MY NEIGHBORS EVERY EVENING. THEY WOULD SAY, 'YOUR JOB MUST BE HARD!'"

Home *Sweet* Home

Three layers cake

(16 slices)

DOUGH

- 13 oz. (375 ml) Guinness beer
- 13 oz. (375 g) soft butter
- 21 oz. (600 g) white sugar
- 4 oz. (125 g) cocoa powder
- 4 eggs
- 11 oz. (300 g) crème fraîche
- 1 teaspoon vanilla extract
- 15 oz. (415 g) flour
- 3/4 oz. bicarbonate of soda

FROSTING

(FOR ONE CAKE)

- 26 oz. (750 g) cream cheese
- 13 oz. (375 g) confectioner's sugar
- 3 1/2 oz. (100 g) cocoa powder

LET'S MAKE THE CAKE!

1

Generously butter three 10-inch springform cake pans. Using three sheets of parchment paper, trace around the bottoms of the pans. Cut out three circles and place them in the bottoms of the pans. Crank up the oven to 350 °F.

2

In a large saucepan, gently heat the beer and butter. Combine the sugar and cocoa powder in a large bowl, then add this mixture into the saucepan while stirring with a whisk. In another bowl, mix the eggs with the crème fraîche and vanilla, then add this mixture into the saucepan while whisking. Combine the flour and bicarbonate of soda in a bowl, then add to the saucepan while stirring well. Divide the dough between the three pans and bake for 15 minutes.

4

Ice ice baby!
Whisk the cream cheese and confectioner's sugar together, then add the cocoa powder. Microwave the frosting for 30 seconds to make it easier to work with. To frost the cake, remove the parchment paper from one of the cake layers, then place it on the base of a springform pan. Frost this layer with a third of the frosting, then flip over the next layer, remove the parchment paper and frost with another third of the frosting. Repeat until the cake and frosting is finished.

If possible, be patient and allow the cake to cool in the refrigerator for two hours before cutting.

3

Wait for the cakes to cool completely and leave in the refrigerator for two hours before frosting if possible.

TAKE A PHOTO
ONCE IT'S
FINISHED
AND POST
IT ON
INSTAGRAM!

Emotion N.35

RAMESH NAIR

Creative Director of Moynat fashion house

CHOCOLATE:

SENSUALITY

FROM

OTHER LANDS

You have probably never thought of it; but he has. Through memories of his native Kerala, Ramesh Nair establishes a link between leather and chocolate.
In the world of House Moynat, among the old trunks bearing letters that suggest distant travels, he ponders this unexpected relationship, combining dedication to a rich and precious trade, with an amazing creative impulse.

CHOCOLATE DOESN'T GROW ON TREES

Ramesh Nair grew up. The climate is not really suitable and cacao beans are not farmed, so no one eats it. Besides,

memories so charming, and Ramesh Nair grew up with a tree in his yard, a tree that was an inseparable part of the structure of his family

He

tells us a simple yet beautiful story. There were no chocolates to be found in Kerala where

no one really knew what it was. Life was centered on the family and nature. The houses stood around a courtyard in which everyone would come and go freely, including animals. It is often an indirect reference that makes

home, his soul, and the intimate setting of his formative years. The tree happened to be a cacao tree.

PARALLELS

66 Chocolate is made like
our creations at Moynat:
with complex simplicity. The art
is in concealing how a simple
chocolate, or a simple small bag,
can represent expertise
and precision. 99

AN INVITATION
_to_ *sensuality*

"I'm always inspired by travel. When I think about chocolate, it immediately evokes images of other lands, of South America, of hard beans whose texture reminds me of leather and which eventually turn into a delicious liquid. I am particularly interested in the transformation of basic materials. Like leather, on which time leaves unique markings that decorate and give life to our everyday items, chocolate also goes through a wonderful transformation. I remember going on a fantastic tour of a chocolaterie in Rocamadour in Quercy. I have memories of the extreme sensuality of it all, images of melted chocolate and waves of aromas hitting our olfactory senses. There is an undeniable link between chocolate and emotion: chocolate invites us to a world of sensuality."

DOUBLE PUNISHMENT

"When I was five years old, I was punished by my mother for fighting with my brother. I was shut in the cellar until I calmed down. While I was there, away from angry looks and reproaches, I found a huge box of chocolate powder, which I proceeded to eat. Having eaten far too much, a strange and very unpleasant feeling overcame me. I was punished twice that day!"

SONIA

Art director and photographer
@souk_and_pix Instagrammer

Who is Sonia?

She is a Paris resident,
full of energy, and leaves you
little photographic messages
that transport you to a world
of poetry and all the sweet things
in life. Sonia shares her passion
for beautifully arranged things
on her @souk_and_pix Instagram
account, showing the charm
of Paris life and attracting the most
discerning of followers. Among
the vibrant colors of spring flowers
and chic summer living, you can
also find plentiful evidence of the
photographer's love of gourmet
foods, including an obvious
weakness for milk chocolate.

COLAT

(A) SLICE *of* tact

"I know the truth now, but I didn't know it back then. My first chocolate memory is something my mother made: a sort of sponge cake cut into slices, with Nutella inside! She would put it in the re-frigerator and then I would devour it without taking a breath! Back then I thought mom was a magician with desserts. In a way she was, although more of an illusionist. But I was obviously fooled!"

CHOCOLATE'S ⟶

"Another memory of my childhood was eating Chocolettis, little milk chocolate squares with hazel-nut praline. They were my first small individual chocolates, which to me felt so much more refined than a bar broken into pieces! Even if they're not actually very refined, they are a fond memory, as if rewinding the film of my high school years. I have so many images when I allow myself these little indulgences, and that is what's so amazing

The BEST MOMENT

"I love milk chocolate with hazelnuts. I eat it every day without fail and for no reason other than I love it! I also love the little excursions I have to do to get supplies: Alain Ducasse, Patrick Roger,

is

and La Maison du Chocolat, where I stock up on incredible milk chocolate rochers. There's no particular time when I like to eat chocolate. Whatever the time, eating chocolate makes me happy, which makes me even happier!"

ALL THE TIME

DECEMBER IS FOR DOUBLE-DIPPING

I usually buy two Advent calendars so I can have two chocolates a day! But who's counting?

← PHOTO ALBUM

about chocolate: it not only reveals its unique flavors, but also triggers lots of images in your head by opening the door to pleasant memories. Taste buds hold the key to accessing lots of past emotions. And in my job as a photographer, I love it when I capture a chocolate macaroon or a half-eaten chocolate so that the image suddenly becomes irresistible!

→ CHOCOLATE BOTH TASTES AND LOOKS DELICIOUS."

APOLLONIA POILÂNE

Baker, President of Poilâne

→

IF YOU ARE A

PARISIAN

THEN YOU KNOW

POILÂNE

SAVOR BREAD

SAVOR CHOCOLATE

AND SAVOR

LIFE!

It is a famous bakery in a country famous for its baguettes. Some like it warm, some like it just plain, but when this celebrated sourdough loaf is adorned with chocolate shavings, it proves that great art can come in the simplest forms. Apollonia Poilâne invites aficionados of tradition to a very personal tasting.

A family history

TO BE A BAKER WHEN YOU LOVE CHOCOLATE IS A REAL BLESSING.

"My father was crazy about chocolate. I remember our family visits to Robert Linxe's boutique in rue de Faubourg Saint-Honoré as a child. Our 'House of Bread' would visit his 'House of Chocolate.' These trips were my first introductions to the art of food tasting. All five of my senses would be stimulated, just like at my family's bakery. And then one day I too became a member of the Club des Croqueurs de Chocolat. I started focusing on the chocolate products our bakery made. I partnered with a chocolatier to bring in better chocolate for our pain au chocolat, one that was better tasting, richer, and molded so that it remained soft and workable even after cooking."

SHARED JOY

↓

" Each time I bite
into a piece of quality chocolate
and a slice of good bread,
my joy grows as I learn
something new about these two
wonderful products,
both of which are the keys
to a healthy body
and mind. "

Braid
with CHOCOLATE *shavings*

Serves one

OF
PREPARATION!

5 min

OF
DELECTATION!

- 1 nice slice of Poilâne bread
- 20 grams of semi-salted butter, churned and salted using traditional methods if possible

- 2 bars of dark chocolate, hard and dry, leave in the refrigerator for 15 minutes before use if necessary

1

Cut a good slice of Poilâne sourdough bread.

2

Spread the slice with semi-salted butter, ensuring the butter is not too chilled so it spreads easily without tearing the bread.

3

Using a small grater, shave off thin slices of dark chocolate from the chocolate bars and scatter all over the butter on your slice of bread.

4

Place the slice of bread on a small plate.

5

Find a comfortable chair

AND SAVOR YOUR WORK OF ART!

1 → OPEN WIDE AND IN IT GOES...

No, no, no, not like that! You need to have small pieces for tasting chocolate properly. It's like tasting wines and any great vintage: you take your time and let your taste buds open up to the flavors and textures. Small amounts at a time. You can even close your eyes and say to yourself: "It's a hard job being a chocolate expert."

TASTE

LIKE

Flavor comes from the quality of the chocolate and not just from its percentage of cocoa solids. Don't just think that 90% cocoa chocolate is the only type that experts will touch. A 64% bar is just as likely to be a grand cru and an award winner.

6 ↑ THE FLAVOR

IN IT FOR THE LONG HAUL: 5 ↓

Good chocolate should linger a long time in the mouth to give enough time for the salivation process to work its magic. Let's not forget, enjoying food is physical!

WHEN YOU'RE A GOOD CHOCOLATE FROM A GOOD FAMILY... → 4

Proper tasting needs regular sips of fresh water. Water won't mask the chocolate's flavor, quenches thirst, and stops you from filling up too fast. After all, it would be a shame to have to bow out early!

2 ← MOUTH WATERING

The perfect time for tasting is between ten and eleven o'clock in the morning. This is when it's been long enough since breakfast, but hunger for lunch has not yet taken ef-

THE PROS

fect. You don't want to be too hungry because this makes you enjoy food for more than its simple taste. Between ten and eleven o'clock, your palate is in a perfect state for critiquing anything the fanciest chefs can throw at you.

...you wait your turn: aromas should line up nicely, not crowd each other like a rabble. You will then experience a succession of evolving flavors coating your palate. You should enjoy a well-paced tour of the chocolate.

3 ↑ CHOCOLATE'S FINEST HOUR

Emotion N. 38

DOROTHÉE MEILICHZON

Interior Designer

CHOCOLATE:

FIRST

→

ON THE MENU

Crossing a small paved courtyard
in Paris' 10th arrondissement, you come across Chzon,
the design agency run by Dorothée Meilichzon.
The atmosphere there is one of surprising calm,
probably a necessary counterbalance
to the frenetic creativity bursting
forth from the minds of the six architects
and designers of this young
and talented team.   →

→ Within this close-knit team, Dorothée primarily works on bespoke projects renovating hotels, bars, and restaurants. She tackles these big projects from start to finish with such passion that she personally designs even the smallest details on the menus. It turns out she takes particular delight in designing profiteroles!

We're always salivating as we work, just thinking of chocolate.

THE ART
of
DESIGNING CHOCOLAT

∨

"I've created small pictograms for dessert menus. Cream puffs, profiteroles, fondant, floating islands... This makes me feel like part of the team and ensures I've completed my mission down to the smallest details."

THE MENU:

A DELICIOUS

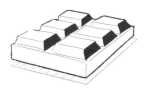

INVITATION

The menu is always
the first thing a customer sees
that incites cravings.

OUR MISSION
WHEN DESIGNING
THEM IS TO TRIGGER
THE URGE
TO ORDER,
TO PROVOKE
IMPATIENCE FOR
THAT MOMENT
WHEN YOU SLIP
A TEASPOON
INTO A PRISTINE
AND DECADENT
DESSERT

Working on
GOOD FOOD
doesn't **FEEL** *like*
WORK !

"Menus are a common element of all food establishments. Each of them inevitably contains chocolate desserts: soft, fluffy chocolate profiteroles with chantilly cream, mango Bavarian cream with Madagascar chocolate... Each menu offers new experiences, new destinations. There are evocative menus, inspiring menus, mouthwatering menus, and ones that revive the classics revisited by modern chefs. My favorite is the giant profiterole made by Thomas Brachet, chef of the Beef Club!"

FRANÇOIS NARS

Founder and Creative Director
of NARS cosmetics

A DAILY RITUAL

For François Nars,
his grandmother's recipes
were his first introduction to the joys of chocolate.
Since then, his daily ritual has always included
visits to fine chocolate makers.
He now lives in New York
and is a well-known regular at the chocolate boutiques of the
city where he can be found several times
a week. As an artist who believes in subtle
blends of boldness and elegance, he is
somewhat of an expert at combinations
that go together. And this includes chocolate.
He knows better than anyone what makes
mouths water and hearts race.

CHOCOLATE
IN MY
private
WORLD

"You're asking people to really open up when asking about their relationship with chocolate. They may be a gourmet or a gourmand, restrained or a complete addict, but you will always find out something very per-sonal about them. For me, chocolate is connected to the private world of my family. Chocolate always brings back these recollections: a cake, a recipe, a drink, something choc-olatey... My grandmother gave me my initiation into the world of chocolate and is responsible for my love of cocoa. She made a mousse to die for. It is to me what a madeleine cake was to Proust, a flavor and aroma I can never forget. It was a dark chocolate mousse, a simple recipe with a unique personal touch added: a few drops of orange blossom water. I re-member the delicacy of this fra-grance. Her mousse was light and airy yet firm, and my grand-mother al-ways presented it in a beautiful crystal bowl so I could see the chocolate through it. I remember scraping the bowls until they were almost spot-less, and grabbing the wooden spoons as soon as I could to lick them dry. And then, if I man-aged to exercise some self-re-straint, I would keep a little mousse for later because it was always better the next day!"

WITHDRAWAL SYMPTOMS

SHAMELESSLY ADDICTED

François Nars does not mince words, and when he admits he is addicted, he's blunt: "I can't live without chocolate. I'm a chocoholic and my week working in New York includes at least three visits to a well-known chocolatier. I'm lucky to live in a city with a La Maison du Chocolat. It sells those praline bites, my biggest weakness.

" I find it very hard when I travel to Los Angeles: I can't find my praline bites there! "

CHOCOLATE IS THE

BEST REMEDY YOU CAN GET

It relaxes me, lets me enter my little bubble and de-stress, all while enjoying myself. After all, there's a certain magic to chocolate, right?"

WITHOUT A PRESCRIPTION.

the_brunswick_brunchie
Musée du Louvre

#lavillegourmande 😳

lebristolparis
Hotel Le Bristol Paris

#latoureiffelacroquer 🤍🐸🤍

CATHERINE, SYLVIE, LAURENT, LUDOVIC...
Behind the scenes at La Maison du Chocolat

How Do You
Exercise
SELF-RESTRAINT?

Understated, generous,
and experts in their field.
They know everything there
is to know about chocolate,
ganache, and the head
chocolatier's secrets.
They offer you tastings of the
latest creations, help you find
the essentials, and set aside
time just for you as soon

as you push open the door
of one of their boutiques.
Delving deeper into the daily
lives of these storekeepers
reveals some wonderful and
charming stories

that show how
La Maison du Chocolat
is a family
unlike any other.

The fans

They are chocoholics but with the unflinching reserve of true gourmets. Many are deeply attached to a particular store and sometimes even to a particular vendor.

They come to La Maison du Chocolat to stock up for three or four days, sometimes for a week.
Their pilgrimage is part of their weekly ritual, written into their agenda as a crucial appointment.

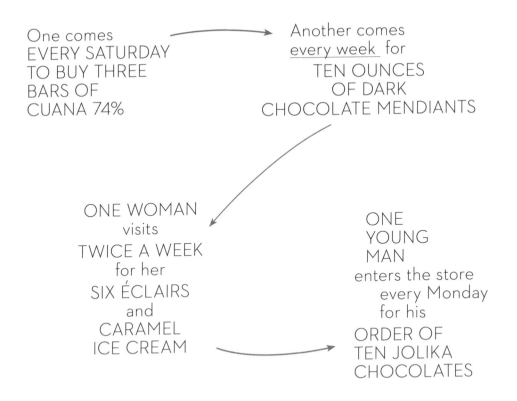

One comes
EVERY SATURDAY
TO BUY THREE
BARS OF
CUANA 74%

Another comes
every week for
TEN OUNCES
OF DARK
CHOCOLATE MENDIANTS

ONE WOMAN
visits
TWICE A WEEK
for her
SIX ÉCLAIRS
and
CARAMEL
ICE CREAM

ONE
YOUNG
MAN
enters the store
every Monday
for his
ORDER OF
TEN JOLIKA
CHOCOLATES

CATHERINE, SYLVIE, LAURENT, LUDOVIC...

Window shopping

What's the difference
between men and women
in a chocolate store?
Everyone agrees:

WOMEN

MEN

Women take their
time to choose
their bite of choice,
hesitating between
two different treats
and then usually
taking them both
in the end.

Men know exactly
what they want:
they walk straight
through the door
and don't look
in the window first.
They are comfortable
in their gluttony!

*When
it comes
to love,*
YOU DON'T
COUNT
THE COST

Large events also produce fascinating stories from La Maison du Chocolat. In one such case, there was a beautiful wedding held at the Grand Hotel in Paris and a large box of chocolates was ordered for each of the 450 guests.

Acknowledgments

A big thank you to all those
who helped in the creation of this book:
the influencers who agreed to confess their glorious addiction
to chocolate with us, the inveterate foodies, the chocobloggers, et al.

We would like to express our gratitude to the entire La Maison du Chocolat team,
Sandrine Huguet and Head Chef Nicolas Cloiseau for their invaluable collaboration
and enthusiasm. Not only did they share their emotions with us,
but also dozens of boxes of chocolates.

And a special thanks to Franck Lacroix, Editor-in-Chief
of *Journal du pâtissier*, whose foreword
to this book wonderfully illustrates
our exploration of chocolate.

lamaisonduchocolat.com

Photography credits

©
Caroline Faccioli
pages 4, 11, 12, 27, 30,31, 34, 35, 48-49, 59, 61, 63, 66,
68, 59, 61, 63, 66, 68, 74, 79, 82-83, 89, 112, 113, 116, 117, 118-119,
120, 126, 141, 147, 148, 152, 153, 173, 178, 182, 187

©
Lindsey Tramuta
page 15

©
Hana Lê Van
page 127

©
Lorenz Bäumer
pages 18-19

©
Laurent Rouvrais
pages 136-137

©
La Maison du Chocolat
page 29

©
Copyright
pages 150-151

©
Astier Nicolas
page 53

©
Jean-François Aloïsi
for MOST
pages 160-161

©
Corinne Decottignies
page 93

©
Ramesh Nair
for Moynat
page 164

©
James Huth:
page 96

©
The Webster
for La Maison du Chocolat
page 107

Instagrams

©

@mayukkuma88 @jotpot19
page 36

@angweddingsny @pandakitchen
page 37

@happycityblog @ alaina_ny
page 45

@theexceptionalwhisky krissharv3y
page 55

@skinnypignyc @sandrinehuguetsicsic
@thepurevida @asako.627
page 71

@seiko_fujii
page 115

@lostncheeseland @grace_ann_pierce
@davidarcamone
page 132

@jo_bazaar
page 133

@souk_and_pix
pages 168-169

@the_brunswick_brunchie @lebristolparis
page 183

Translations

Pierre Hermé
The "Robert" Chocolate Bonbon
Page 63:

- 1/2 in. (12 mm) single-origin Belize 64% ganache
- 5/64 in. (2 mm) amaranth chocolate
- Dark chocolate coating
- square + red fork mark

Single-origin Belize 64% ganache
- 23 oz. (660 g) cream
- 25 oz. (700 g) single-origin Belize 64% Couverture chocolate
- 1 1/2 oz. (40 g) 60 DE glucose syrup
- 4 oz. (115 g) butter

Amaranth chocolate
- 18 oz. (500 g) single-origin Belize 64% couverture chocolate
- 3 oz. (80 g) clarified butter
- 2 oz. (55 g) toasted amaranth (320 °F for 20 min)

Spread a 5/64 in. (2 mm) layer, let it rest/crystallize, then pour a 1/2 in. (12 mm) layer of ganache on top. Cut into 1 in. x 1/2 in. (30 mm x 15 mm) squares

Sketches by Ines de la Fressange
Page 65:
Almighty one, please invent a new chocolate-based diet!
Page 66 :
I'm ashamed of my taste in chocolate: sweet mass-produced candy bars!
So I chose to draw you some cartoons instead. Or should I say "cacao-toons"!
Warm regards, Ines de la Fressange
Page 67 :
- Me, magnesium deficient? Never!
- How did you know it was my favorite chocolate?
- If I told you the truth about my diet, I'd be lynched!
- A chocolate bar is a girl magnet!

James Huth - Chocoholic 714 C - 256 -
Police Department
Page 96 :
- You prefer chocolate to vanilla.
- You can't give someone a box of chocolates without buying one for yourself.
- You have finished a 1-pint tub of chocolate ice cream in front of the TV.
- You put chocolate sauce on top of your ice cream.
- You are willing to travel more than 6 miles to find chocolate.
- You always add chocolate chips to your chocolate cookies.
- You can't ever just take one chocolate from the box when it's passed around.
- You prefer chocolate cake batter to the cooked cake.
- You immediately pick out the chocolate desserts on a menu.
- You only go to hotels for the chocolates on the pillows.
- You're not good company until you've had your daily dose of chocolate.
- You don't care what color M&Ms you get as long as you can eat some.
If you have checked off two or more items on this list, you are strongly advised to immediately visit your local chocolate store.

Editorial coordination:
Laure Lamendin

Design and layout:
aplus.design

Translation from original French text:
Primoscrib (R. Latchford)

Published by Éditions de la Martinière, an imprint of EDLM
©2017 Éditions de la Martinière
Library of Congress Control Number: 2016962809

ISBN: 978-1-4197-2515-9

Color separation: IGS
Printed and bound in 2017 in Slovenia
10 9 8 7 6 5 4 3 2 1

ABRAMS The Art of Books
115 West 18th Street, New York, NY 10011
abramsbooks.com